Learning Python Design Patterns

A practical and fast-paced guide exploring
Python design patterns

Gennadiy Zlobin

[PACKT] open source ✹

PUBLISHING   community experience distilled

BIRMINGHAM - MUMBAI

Learning Python Design Patterns

First published: November 2013

Production Reference: 1181113

Published by Packt Publishing Ltd.
Livery Place
35 Livery Street
Birmingham B3 2PB, UK.

ISBN 978-1-78328-337-8

www.packtpub.com

Cover Image by Aniket Sawant (aniket_sawant_photography@hotmail.com)

Credits

Author
Gennadiy Zlobin

Reviewers
David Corne

Kamilla Holanda Crozara

Sakis Kasampalis

Acquisition Editors
Kunal Parikh

Llewellyn Rozario

Commissioning Editor
Sruthi Kutty

Technical Editors
Vrinda Nitesh Bhosale

Rohit Kumar Singh

Copy Editors
Alisha Aranha

Sarang Chari

Janbal Dharmaraj

Dipti Kapadia

Gladson Monteiro

Karuna Narayanan

Project Coordinator
Suraj Bist

Proofreader
Simran Bhogal

Indexer
Hemangini Bari

Graphics
Abhinash Sahu

Production Coordinator
Nitesh Thakur

Cover Work
Nitesh Thakur

About the Author

Gennadiy Zlobin works as Lead Software Engineer and Technical Leader in the Russian music service, `Zvooq.ru`. His current employer is Zvooq Ltd. He has been using Python as the primary language for more than 4 years, enjoying its elegance and power every day. His professional interests include high-load software architectures, good engineering practices, Android OS, and natural language processing.

Previously, he worked for the company that had the first search engine in Russia, called Rambler. He was engaged in airline tickets' meta search service and Rambler's index page.

I would like to thank my wife, Jane, for her patience and support.
I really appreciate it.

I am also grateful to my parents, Galina and Vitaliy for believing
in me. I love all of you.

About the Reviewers

David Corne is a professional Software Engineer based in Birmingham, UK. He works for an engineering company that makes CAD/CAM software. The application he is working on is written in C++ with a C# view layer in order to use WPF.

However, he has a keen interest in Python. He has made many varied applications in Python. These range from a real-time updating editor for Markdown, to a utility for dice rolling, and PDF reading.

Kamilla Holanda Crozara is in her last year of college and is studying Software Engineering and works at National Institute of Standards and Technology as a Guest Researcher. She started to learn Python around two years ago, and it's her favorite language although she has some experience with C, Java, and Perl languages. She's a Linux user and has a special interest in contributing towards open source projects.

Sakis Kasampalis is based in the Netherlands, where he currently works as a Software Engineer for a location-based content B2B provider. When he is not writing C++ and Rails code for a living, Sakis enjoys playing with his mbed microcontroller and studying about programming, software engineering, and operating systems.

He is not dogmatic about particular programming languages and tools; his principle is that the right tool should be used for the right job. One of his favorite tools is Python because he finds it very productive.

Among his FOSS activities is maintaining a GitHub repository related to implementing design patterns in Python, which is available at `https://github.com/faif/python-patterns`.

www.PacktPub.com

Support files, eBooks, discount offers and more

You might want to visit www.PacktPub.com for support files and downloads related to your book.

Did you know that Packt offers eBook versions of every book published, with PDF and ePub files available? You can upgrade to the eBook version at www.PacktPub.com and as a print book customer, you are entitled to a discount on the eBook copy. Get in touch with us at service@packtpub.com for more details.

At www.PacktPub.com, you can also read a collection of free technical articles, sign up for a range of free newsletters and receive exclusive discounts and offers on Packt books and eBooks.

http://PacktLib.PacktPub.com

Do you need instant solutions to your IT questions? PacktLib is Packt's online digital book library. Here, you can access, read and search across Packt's entire library of books.

Why Subscribe?

- Fully searchable across every book published by Packt
- Copy and paste, print and bookmark content
- On demand and accessible via web browser

Free Access for Packt account holders

If you have an account with Packt at www.PacktPub.com, you can use this to access PacktLib today and view nine entirely free books. Simply use your login credentials for immediate access.

Table of Contents

Preface   **1**

Chapter 1: Model-View-Controller   **7**

  Model – the knowledge of the application   8
  View – the appearance of knowledge   8
  Controller – the glue between the model and view   9
  Benefits of using the MVC   10
  Implementation in Python   10
  Summary   16

Chapter 2: Creating Only One Object with the Singleton Pattern   **17**

  A module-level singleton   18
  A classic singleton   19
  The borg singleton   20
  Implementation in Python   21
  Summary   26

Chapter 3: Building Factories to Create Objects   **27**

  The Factory Method   29
    Advantages of using the Factory Method pattern   30
    The Factory Method implementation   30
  Abstract Factory   35
    Advantages of using the Abstract Factory pattern   36
    Abstract Factory implementation   37
  Abstract Factory versus Factory Method   40
  Summary   41

Chapter 4: The Facade Design Pattern   **43**

  The Facade design pattern   43
    Problems solved by the Facade pattern   45
    Advantages of the Facade design pattern   45

Facades in Python's standard library	**45**
Implementation in Python	**47**
Summary	**51**
Chapter 5: Facilitating Object Communication with Proxy and Observer Patterns	**53**
Proxy design pattern	**54**
Problems solved by the Proxy pattern	54
The use of the Proxy pattern	55
Advantages and disadvantages of the Proxy design pattern	55
Implementation in Python	55
Observer design pattern	**59**
Problems solved by the Observer pattern	60
Use of the Observer pattern	61
Advantages of the Observer pattern	61
Implementation in Python	61
Summary	**65**
Chapter 6: Encapsulating Calls with the Command Pattern	**67**
Command Pattern terminology	**68**
Use cases of the Command design pattern	**69**
Advantages and disadvantages of the Command design pattern	**69**
Implementation in Python	**70**
Summary	**75**
Chapter 7: Redefining Algorithms with the Template Method	**77**
The Template Method design pattern	**77**
The benefits of the Template Method design pattern	78
Using hooks	79
Implementation in Python	**79**
Summary	**85**
Index	**87**

Preface

Python is a great programming language, elegant and concise, and at the same time, very powerful. It has all the essential object-oriented features and can be used to implement design patterns. A design pattern is a general reusable solution to a commonly occurring problem within a given context. In everyday work, a programmer faces issues that have been solved so many times in the past by other developers that they have evolved common patterns to solve them.

The design pattern is not a concrete step to solve a problem, such as an algorithm; it is rather a practice or a description of how to solve a problem that can be used in different situations and implemented in different languages.

The design pattern accelerates the development process, providing a proven practice to solve some type of problem. It is often more preferable than using an unproven one because invisible problems often occur during the implementation, and the solving of unforeseen problems slows down the development dramatically.

Besides that, it's a tool of communication between programmers. It's much easier to say, "We use here the observer design pattern" rather than describing what the code actually does.

Studying design patterns is a good next step on the road to becoming a great developer, and this book is a good jumpstart.

What this book covers

Chapter 1, *Model-View-Controller*, describes what the model, view, and controller are, how to use them together, and ends with the implementation of a very simple URL shortening service.

Chapter 2, Creating Only One Object with the Singleton Pattern, describes ways to create a class whose instantiated object will only be one throughout the lifecycle of an application.

Chapter 3, Building Factories to Create Objects, describes the simple factory, Factory Method, Abstract Factory patterns, and how to use them to separate object creation.

Chapter 4, The Facade Design Pattern, is about simplifying the interface of a complex subsystem to facilitate the development.

Chapter 5, Facilitating Object Communication with Proxy and Observer Patterns, is a pattern for implementing a publisher-subscriber model and a proxy, which provides an object that controls access to another object.

Chapter 6, Encapsulating Calls with the Command Pattern, describes a pattern that encapsulates an action and its parameters.

Chapter 7, Redefining Algorithms with the Template Method, is about a pattern that provides the ability to create variations of the algorithm with minimum modifications.

What you need for this book

You will require a Python 2.7 installation. It's usually available out of the box on most Unix and Linux distributives and can be downloaded and installed on Windows from `http://python.org/`.

Who this book is for

This book is for developers with an intermediate Python knowledge who want to make learning design patterns their next step in their development career.

Conventions

In this book, you will find a number of styles of text that distinguish between different kinds of information. Here are some examples of these styles, and an explanation of their meaning.

Code words in text are shown as follows: "As we see, Atom uses the `<entry>` tag instead of the `<item>` tag, link is stored in attribute instead of text node."

A block of code is set as follows:

```
<?xml version="1.0" encoding="ISO-8859-1" ?>
<rss version="2.0">
  <channel>
    <title>A RSS example</title>
    <link>http://example.com</link>
    <description>Description of RSS example</description>
    <item>
      <title>The first news</title>
      <link>http://example.com/first</link>
      <description>Some description of the first news</description>
    </item>
    <item>
      <guid>urn:uuid:1225c695-cfb8-4ebb-aaaa-80da344efa6a</id>
      <title>The second news</title>
      <link>example.com/second</link>
      <description>Some description of the second
        news</description>
      <pubDate>Wed, 30 Sep 2013 13:00:00 GMT</pubDate>
    </item>
  </channel>
</rss>
```

When we wish to draw your attention to a particular part of a code block, the relevant lines or items are set in bold:

```
{
  "main": {
    "temp": 280.28,
  },
  "dt_txt": "2013-10-24 00:00:00"
}
```

Any command-line input or output is written as follows:

```
$ python controller.py
```

New terms and **important words** are shown in bold as: "The other frequent use is to pass the **Subject** instance itself instead of data."

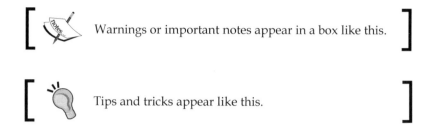

[Warnings or important notes appear in a box like this.   ]

[Tips and tricks appear like this.   ]

Reader feedback

Feedback from our readers is always welcome. Let us know what you think about this book—what you liked or may have disliked. Reader feedback is important for us to develop titles that you really get the most out of.

To send us general feedback, simply send an e-mail to feedback@packtpub.com, and mention the book title via the subject of your message.

If there is a topic that you have expertise in and you are interested in either writing or contributing to a book, see our author guide on www.packtpub.com/authors.

Customer support

Now that you are the proud owner of a Packt book, we have a number of things to help you to get the most from your purchase.

Downloading the example code

You can download the example code files for all Packt books you have purchased from your account at http://www.packtpub.com. If you purchased this book elsewhere, you can visit http://www.packtpub.com/support and register to have the files e-mailed directly to you.

Errata

Although we have taken every care to ensure the accuracy of our content, mistakes do happen. If you find a mistake in one of our books—maybe a mistake in the text or the code—we would be grateful if you would report this to us. By doing so, you can save other readers from frustration and help us improve subsequent versions of this book. If you find any errata, please report them by visiting `http://www.packtpub.com/submit-errata`, selecting your book, clicking on the **errata submission form** link, and entering the details of your errata. Once your errata are verified, your submission will be accepted and the errata will be uploaded on our website, or added to any list of existing errata, under the Errata section of that title. Any existing errata can be viewed by selecting your title from `http://www.packtpub.com/support`.

Piracy

Piracy of copyright material on the Internet is an ongoing problem across all media. At Packt, we take the protection of our copyright and licenses very seriously. If you come across any illegal copies of our works, in any form, on the Internet, please provide us with the location address or website name immediately so that we can pursue a remedy.

Please contact us at `copyright@packtpub.com` with a link to the suspected pirated material.

We appreciate your help in protecting our authors, and our ability to bring you valuable content.

Questions

You can contact us at `questions@packtpub.com` if you are having a problem with any aspect of the book, and we will do our best to address it.

1
Model-View-Controller

Many applications start from something small, such as several hundred lines of code prototype of a toy application written in one evening. When you add new features and the application code clutters, it becomes much harder to understand how it works and to modify it, especially for a newcomer. **The Model-View-Controller (MVC)** pattern serves as the basis for software architecture that will be easily maintained and modified.

The main idea of MVC is about separating an application into three parts: model, view, and controller. There is an easy way to understand MVC — the model is the data and its business logic, the view is the window on the screen, and the controller is the glue between the two.

While the view and controller depend on the model, the model is independent of the presentation or the controller. This is a key feature of the division. It allows you to work with the model, and hence, the business logic of the application, regardless of the visual presentation.

The following diagram shows the flow of interaction between the user, controller, model, and view. Here, a user makes a request to the application and the controller does the initial processing. After that it manipulates the model, creating, updating, or deleting some data there. The model returns some result to the controller, that passes the result to view, which renders data to the user.

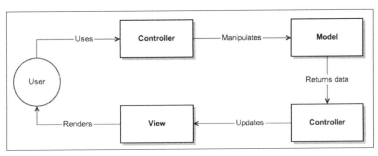

The MVC pattern gained wide popularity in web development. Many Python web frameworks, such as web2py, Pyramid, Django (uses a flavor of MVC called MVP), Giotto, and Kiss use it.

Let's review key components of the MVC pattern in more detail.

Model – the knowledge of the application

The model is a cornerstone of the application because, while the view and controller depend on the model, the model is independent of the presentation or the controller.

The model provides knowledge: data, and how to work with that data. The model has a state and methods for changing its state but does not contain information on how this knowledge can be visualized.

This independence makes working independently, covering the model with tests and substituting the controllers/views without changing the business logic of an application.

The model is responsible for maintaining the integrity of the program's data, because if that gets corrupted then it's game over for everyone.

The following are recommendations for working with models:

- Strive to perform the following for models:
    - Create data models and interface of work with them
    - Validate data and report all errors to the controller

- Avoid working directly with the user interface

View – the appearance of knowledge

View receives data from the model through the controller and is responsible for its visualization. It should not contain complex logic; all such logic should go to the models and controllers.

If you need to change the method of visualization, for example, if you need your web application to be rendered differently depending on whether the user is using a mobile phone or desktop browser, you can change the view accordingly. This can include HTML, XML, console views, and so on.

The recommendation for working with views are as follows:

- Strive to perform the following for views:
    - ○ Try to keep them simple; use only simple comparisons and loops
- Avoid doing the following in views:
    - ○ Accessing the database directly
    - ○ Using any logic other than loops and conditional statements (if-then-else) because the separation of concerns requires all such complex logic to be performed in models

Controller – the glue between the model and view

The direct responsibility of the controllers is to receive data from the request and send it to other parts of the system. Only in this case, the controller is "thin" and is intended only as a bridge (glue layer) between the individual components of the system.

Let's look at the following recommendations for working with controllers:

- Strive to perform the following in controllers:
    - ○ Pass data from user requests to the model for processing, retrieving and saving the data
    - ○ Pass data to views for rendering
    - ○ Handle all request errors and errors from models
- Avoid the following in controllers:
    - ○ Render data
    - ○ Work with the database and business logic directly

Thus, in one statement:

We need *smart* models, *thin* controllers, and *dumb* views.

Benefits of using the MVC

MVC brings a lot of positive attributes to your software, including the following:

1. Decomposition allows you to logically split the application into three relatively independent parts with loose coupling and will decrease its complexity.

2. Developers typically specialize in one area, for example, a developer might create a user interface or modify the business logic. Thus, it's possible to limit their area of responsibility to only some part of code.

3. MVC makes it possible to change visualization, thus modifying the view without changes in the business logic.

4. MVC makes it possible to change business logic, thus modifying the model without changes in visualization.

5. MVC makes it possible to change the response to a user action (clicking on the button with the mouse, data entry) without changing the implementation of views; it is sufficient to use a different controller.

Implementation in Python

For a practical example, we'll create a very simple but working URL shortening service with a Flask micro framework that is developed by Pocoo.

Flask is a micro framework that is intended to create simple and short applications. It provides API for handling typical web-development tasks. On the other hand, it does not have object-relational mapping, form validations, and other features typical to bigger frameworks such as Django or Pyramid. Flask is very expansible with third-party libraries and modules. It does not use MVC out of the box, but let's us take advantage of its high customization and allows us to use the MVC pattern in Flask.

First, you should have Flask installed. Any one of the following commands should be sufficient to install Flask:

- `$ sudo pip install Flask`
- `$ sudo easy_install Flask`

Let's create a model that contains all our data operations and business logic.

We create the `Url` class that represents the URL entity. This class will have two properties: `full_url` and `short_url`. If the user accessed our website with a short URL, we will find the `Url` instance using `short_url` and redirect the user there.

The `shorten` method provides an interface method for the controller. The controller will call this method by passing the full URL. The model will generate a short URL and will save it for further retrieval.

The `get_by_short_url` method provides the second interface method for the controller. The controller will call this method by passing the `short_url` value, and the model will retrieve the `Url` instance with `short_url` and return it to the controller.

The other methods are the helpers to process the business logic, for example, to generate a short URL, as shown in the following code, in order or to save the `Url` instance and retrieve it from storage.

The code for `models.py` is as follows:

```python
import pickle

class Url(object):
    @classmethod
    def shorten(cls, full_url):
        """Shortens full url."""

        # Create an instance of Url class
        instance = cls()
        instance.full_url = full_url
        instance.short_url = instance.__create_short_url()
        Url.__save_url_mapping(instance)
        return instance

    @classmethod
    def get_by_short_url(cls, short_url):
        """Returns Url instance, corresponding to short_url."""
        url_mapping = Url.load_url_mapping()
        return url_mapping.get(short_url)

    def __create_short_url(self):
        """Creates short url, saves it and returns it."""
        last_short_url = Url.__load_last_short_url()
        short_url = self.__increment_string(last_short_url)
        Url.__save_last_short_url(short_url)
        return short_url

    def __increment_string(self, string):
        """Increments string, that is:
            a -> b
```

```
        z -> aa
        az -> ba
        empty string -> a

    """
    if string == '':
      return 'a'

    last_char = string[-1]

    if last_char != 'z':
      return string[:-1] + chr(ord(last_char) + 1)

    return self.__increment_string(string[:-1]) + 'a'

  @staticmethod
  def __load_last_short_url():
    """Returns last generated short url."""
    try:
      return pickle.load(open("last_short.p", "rb"))
    except IOError:
      return ''

  @staticmethod
  def __save_last_short_url(url):
    """Saves last generated short url."""
    pickle.dump(url, open("last_short.p", "wb"))

  @staticmethod
  def __load_url_mapping():
    """Returns short_url to Url instance mapping."""
    try:
      return pickle.load(open("short_to_url.p", "rb"))
    except IOError:
      return {}

  @staticmethod
  def __save_url_mapping(instance):
    """Saves short_url to Url instance mapping."""
    short_to_url = Url.__load_url_mapping()
    short_to_url[instance.short_url] = instance
    pickle.dump(short_to_url, open("short_to_url.p", "wb"))
```

Let's create our view. The view is responsible for rendering data from the model to the end users, and here we have several options. The first option is to create another class where every method is responsible to perform simple logic and call templates to render.

The second option is to use the templates directly. Flask uses the Jinja2 template engine that provides use of template tags. For example, to perform comparisons, we can use the following:

```
{% if var == True %}
...//some code
{% endif %}
```

Jinja2 also allows us to use passed variables from the controller, iterate loops, and inherit one template from another. So let's use this smart template engine as views, and write a couple of views to render to the user.

Create a `views` directory and the `main_page.html` and `success.html` files should be created in `views` directory.

The `main_page.html` file is the main page of the application that has a form with an input field to enter the full URL of website and the `submit` button, when clicked, sends full URL to controller.

The code for `main_page.html` is as follows:

```
<form action="/shorten/">
  <label>
  <input type="text" name="url" value="" />
    Link to shorten
  </label>
  <input type="submit" value="OK"/>
</form>
```

The `success.html` page is a view for rendering a success message with a short version of the URL that the user asked to shorten.

The code for the `success.html` page looks like this:

```
Congratulations! <br />
Your url: {{ short_url }}
```

The controller will need to process three types of requests:

- Render the main page
- Process the request to shorten the URL
- Process the request to convert the URL from short to full and then redirect it

In the following code, the `process` function renders the main page. Please note how it works: it takes the full URL from the request arguments, passes them to the model, and then passes the returned data to the view.

The `redirect_to_full_url` method takes the short URL from the requests, gets the full URL from the model, makes very simple validations, and redirects the user to the full URL.

The code for `controller.py` is as follows:

```python
# Redirect function is used to forward user to full url if he came
# from shortened
# Request is used to encapsulate HTTP request. It will contain request
# methods, request arguments and other related information
# from flask import redirect, render_template, request, Flask
# from werkzeug.exceptions import BadRequest, NotFound

import models

# Initialize Flask application
app = Flask(__name__, template_folder='views')


@app.route("/")
def index():
    """Renders main page."""
    return render_template('main_page.html')

@app.route("/shorten/")
def shorten():
    """Returns short_url of requested full_url."""
    # Validate user input
    full_url = request.args.get('url')
    if not full_url:
        raise BadRequest()

    # Model returns object with short_url property
    url_model = models.Url.shorten(full_url)
    url_model.short_url

    # Pass data to view and call its render method
    short_url = request.host + '/' + url_model.short_url
    return render_template('success.html', short_url=short_url)
```

```
@app.route('/<path:path>')
def redirect_to_full(path=''):
    """Gets short url and redirects user to corresponding full url if
found."""
    # Model returns object with full_url property
    url_model = models.Url.get_by_short_url(path)

    # Validate model return
    if not url_model:
        raise NotFound()

    return redirect(url_model.full_url)

if __name__ == "__main__":
    app.run(debug=True)
```

To run the application, place these files in one directory, open the terminal, run the following command, and go to `http://127.0.0.1:5000` in your browser:

```
$ python controller.py
```

You will get a view similar to the following screenshot:

Now fill the form with a URL, for example, `http://www.packtpub.com`, click on **OK**, and see its shortened version.

If you copy its shortened version and paste it to your browser, you should be redirected to `www.packtub.com`.

Summary

It is important to separate the areas of responsibility to maintain loose coupling and for the maintainability of the software. MVC divides the application into three relatively independent parts: model, view, and controller. The model is all about knowledge, data, and business logic. The view is about presentation to the end users, and it's important to keep it simple. The controller is the glue between the model and the view, and it's important to keep it thin. In the practical example, you created a simple but fully-functional URL shortening service with the MVC pattern.

In this chapter, you used the pickle module for conserving the application data. But what if you were to use the database to do it? You would need to connect to the database. Connecting to the database is a heavy operation, so it is better to connect to it once and then just use this connection during the working of the application. In the next chapter, you will learn about the Singleton pattern that allows you to create only one object even if the instantiation has been done several times.

2

Creating Only One Object with the Singleton Pattern

There are situations where you need to create only one instance of data throughout the lifetime of a program. This can be a class instance, a list, or a dictionary, for example. The creation of a second instance is undesirable. This can result in logical errors or malfunctioning of the program. The design pattern that allows you to create only one instance of data is called **singleton**. In this chapter, you will learn about module-level, classic, and borg singletons; you'll also learn about how they work, when to use them, and build a two-threaded web crawler that uses a singleton to access the shared resource.

Singleton is the best candidate when the requirements are as follows:

- If you need to control concurrent access to a shared resource
- If you need a global point of access for the resource from multiple or different parts of the system
- If you need to have only one object

Some typical use cases of a singleton are:

- The logging class and its subclasses (global point of access for the logging class to send messages to log)
- Printer spooler (your application should only have a single instance of the spooler in order to avoid having a conflicting request for the same resource)
- Managing a connection to a database
- File manager
- Retrieving and storing information on external configuration files
- Read-only singletons storing some global states (user language, time, time zone, application path, and so on)

There are several ways to implement singletons. We will look at a module-level singleton, classic singletons, and a borg singleton.

A module-level singleton

All modules are singletons by nature because of Python's module importing steps:

1. Check whether a module is already imported.

2. If yes, return it.

3. If not, find a module, initialize it, and return it.

4. Initializing a module means executing code, including all module-level assignments. When you import the module for the first time, all initializations are done; however, if you try to import the module for the second time, Python will return the initialized module. Thus, the initialization will not be done, and you get a previously imported module with all of its data

So, if you want to quickly make a singleton, use the following code and keep the shared data as the module attribute:

```
singletone.py:
only_one_var = "I'm only one var"

module1.py:
import single tone
print singleton.only_one_var
singletone.only_one_var += " after modification"
import module2

module2.py:
import singletone
print singleton.only_one_var
```

Here, if you try to import a global variable in a `singleton.py` module and change its value in the `module1.py` module, `module2.py` will recieve a changed variable.

This function is quick and sometimes is all you need; however, we need to consider the following points:

- It's pretty error-prone. For example, if you happen to forget the global statements, variables local to the function will be created and the module's variables won't be changed, which is not what you want.

- It's ugly, especially if you have a lot of objects that should remain as singletons.
- It pollutes the module namespace with unnecessary variables.
- They don't permit lazy allocation and initialization; all global variables will be loaded during the module import process.
- It's not possible to reuse the code because you cannot use the inheritance.
- It has no special methods and no object-oriented programming benefits at all.

A classic singleton

In a classic singleton in Python, we check whether an instance is already created. If it is created, we return it; otherwise, we create a new instance, assign it to a class attribute, and return it.

Let's try to create a dedicated singleton class:

```
class Singleton(object):
  def __new__(cls):
    if not hasattr(cls, 'instance'):
      cls.instance = super(Singleton, cls).__new__(cls)
    return cls.instance
```

Here, before creating the instance, we check for the special __new__ method that is called right before __init__ if we had created an instance earlier. If not, we create a new instance; otherwise, we return the already created instance.

Let's check how it works:

```
>>> singleton = Singleton()
>>> another_singleton = Singleton()
>>> singleton is another_singleton
True
>>> singleton.only_one_var = "I'm only one var"
>>> another_singleton.only_one_var
I'm only one var
```

Try to subclass the Singleton class with another one:

```
class Child(Singleton):
  pass
```

If some class is a successor of Singleton, all successor's instances should also be the instances of Singleton, thus sharing its states. But this doesn't work, as illustrated in the following code:

```
>>> child = Child()
>>> child is singleton
>>> False
```

```
>>> child.only_one_var
AttributeError: Child instance has no attribute 'only_one_var'
```

To avoid this situation, the borg singleton is used.

The borg singleton

Borg is also known as **monostate**. In the borg pattern, all of the instances are different, but they share the same state.

In the following code, the shared state is maintained in the _shared_state attribute. And all new instances of the Borg class will have this state as defined in the __new__ class method:

```
class Borg(object):
  _shared_state = {}

  def __new__(cls, *args, **kwargs):

    obj = super(Borg, cls).__new__(cls, *args, **kwargs)
    obj.__dict__ = cls._shared_state
    return obj
```

Generally, Python stores the instance state in the __dict__ dictionary and when instantiated normally, every instance will have its own __dict__. But, here we deliberately assign the class variable _shared_state to all of the created instances.

The following code shows how it works with subclassing:

```
class Child(Borg):
  pass
>>> borg = Borg()
>>> another_borg = Borg()
>>> borg is another_borg
False
>>> child = Child()
>>> borg.only_one_var = "I'm the only one var"
>>> child.only_one_var
I'm the only one var
```

So, despite the fact that you can't compare objects by their identity, using the is statement, all child objects share the parents' state.

If you want to have a class that is a descendant of the Borg class but has a different state, you can reset shared_state as follows:

```
class AnotherChild(Borg):
  _shared_state = {}

>>> another_child = AnotherChild()
>>> another_child.only_one_var
AttributeError: AnotherChild instance has no attribute 'shared_state'
```

It is up to you to decide which type of singleton should be used. If you expect that your singleton will not be inherited, you can choose the classic singleton; otherwise, it's better to stick with borg.

Implementation in Python

As a practical example, we'll create a simple web crawler that scans a website you open on it, follows all the links that lead to the same website but to other pages, and downloads all of the images it'll find.

To do this, we'll need two functions: a function that scans a website for links that lead to other pages to build a set of pages to visit, and a function that scans a page for images and downloads them.

To make it quicker, we'll download images in two threads. These two threads should not interfere with each other, so don't scan pages if another thread has already scanned them, and don't download images that are already downloaded.

So, a set with downloaded images and scanned web pages will be a shared resource for our application, and we'll keep it in a singleton instance.

In this example, you will need a library for parsing and screen scraping websites named `BeautifulSoup` and an HTTP client library, `httplib2`. It should be sufficient to install both with either of the following commands:

- `$ sudo pip install BeautifulSoup httplib2`
- `$ sudo easy_install BeautifulSoup httplib2`

First of all, we'll create a `Singleton` class. Let's use the classic singleton in the following example:

```
import httplib2
import os
import re
import threading
import urllib
from urlparse import urlparse, urljoin
```

```
from BeautifulSoup import BeautifulSoup

class Singleton(object):
  def __new__(cls):
    if not hasattr(cls, 'instance'):
       cls.instance = super(Singleton, cls).__new__(cls)
    return cls.instance
```

It will return the singleton objects to all parts of the code that request it.

Next, we'll create a class for creating a thread. In this thread, we'll download images from the website:

```
class ImageDownloaderThread(threading.Thread):
  """A thread for downloading images in parallel."""
  def __init__(self, thread_id, name, counter):
    threading.Thread.__init__(self)
    self.name = name

  def run(self):
    print 'Starting thread ', self.name
    download_images(self.name)
    print 'Finished thread ', self.name
```

The following function traverses the website using BFS algorithm, finds links, and adds them to a set for further downloading. We are able to specify the maximum links to follow if the website is too large:

```
def traverse_site(max_links=10):
  link_parser_singleton = Singleton()

  # While we have pages to parse in queue
  while link_parser_singleton.queue_to_parse:
    # If collected enough links to download images, return
    if len(link_parser_singleton.to_visit) == max_links:
      return

    url = link_parser_singleton.queue_to_parse.pop()

    http = httplib2.Http()
    try:
      status, response = http.request(url)
    except Exception:
      continue
```

```
# Skip if not a web page
if status.get('content-type') != 'text/html':
  continue

# Add the link to queue for downloading images
link_parser_singleton.to_visit.add(url)
print 'Added', url, 'to queue'

bs = BeautifulSoup(response)

for link in BeautifulSoup.findAll(bs, 'a'):

  link_url = link.get('href')

  # <img> tag may not contain href attribute
  if not link_url:
    continue

  parsed = urlparse(link_url)

  # If link follows to external webpage, skip it
  if parsed.netloc and parsed.netloc != parsed_root.netloc:
    continue

  # Construct a full url from a link which can be relative
  link_url = (parsed.scheme or parsed_root.scheme) + '://' +
(parsed.netloc or parsed_root.netloc) + parsed.path or ''

  # If link was added previously, skip it
  if link_url in link_parser_singleton.to_visit:
    continue

  # Add a link for further parsing
  link_parser_singleton.queue_to_parse = [link_url] + link_parser_
singleton.queue_to_parse
```

The following function downloads images from the last web resource page in the singleton.to_visit queue and saves it to the img directory. Here, we use a singleton for synchronizing shared data, which is a set of pages to visit between two threads:

```
def download_images(thread_name):
  singleton = Singleton()
  # While we have pages where we have not download images
  while singleton.to_visit:
```

```
    url = singleton.to_visit.pop()

    http = httplib2.Http()
    print thread_name, 'Starting downloading images from', url

    try:
        status, response = http.request(url)
    except Exception:
        continue

    bs = BeautifulSoup(response)

    # Find all <img> tags
    images = BeautifulSoup.findAll(bs, 'img')

    for image in images:
        # Get image source url which can be absolute or relative
        src = image.get('src')
        # Construct a full url. If the image url is relative,
        # it will be prepended with webpage domain.
        # If the image url is absolute, it will remain as is
        src = urljoin(url, src)

        # Get a base name, for example 'image.png' to name file locally
        basename = os.path.basename(src)

        if src not in singleton.downloaded:
            singleton.downloaded.add(src)
            print 'Downloading', src
            # Download image to local filesystem
            urllib.urlretrieve(src, os.path.join('images', basename))

print thread_name, 'finished downloading images from', url
```

Our client code is as follows:

```
if __name__ == '__main__':
  root = 'http://python.org'

  parsed_root = urlparse(root)

  singleton = Singleton()
  singleton.queue_to_parse = [root]
  # A set of urls to download images from
  singleton.to_visit = set()
  # Downloaded images
  singleton.downloaded = set()

  traverse_site()

  # Create images directory if not exists
  if not os.path.exists('images'):
    os.makedirs('images')

  # Create new threads
  thread1 = ImageDownloaderThread(1, "Thread-1", 1)
  thread2 = ImageDownloaderThread(2, "Thread-2", 2)

  # Start new Threads
  thread1.start()
  thread2.start()
```

Run a crawler using the following command:

```
$ python crawler.py
```

You should get the following output (your output may vary because the order in which the threads access resources is not predictable):

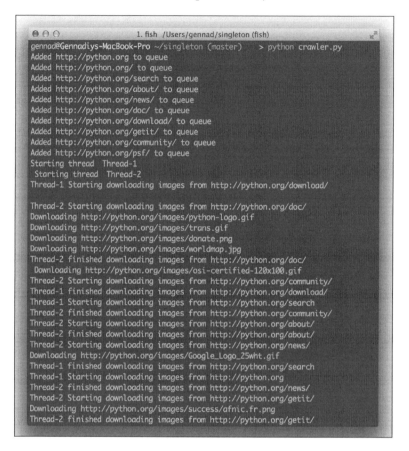

```
● ○ ○                    1. fish  /Users/gennad/singleton (fish)
gennad@Gennadiys-MacBook-Pro ~/singleton (master)  > python crawler.py
Added http://python.org to queue
Added http://python.org/ to queue
Added http://python.org/search to queue
Added http://python.org/about/ to queue
Added http://python.org/news/ to queue
Added http://python.org/doc/ to queue
Added http://python.org/download/ to queue
Added http://python.org/getit/ to queue
Added http://python.org/community/ to queue
Added http://python.org/psf/ to queue
Starting thread  Thread-1
 Starting thread  Thread-2
Thread-1 Starting downloading images from http://python.org/download/

Thread-2 Starting downloading images from http://python.org/doc/
Downloading http://python.org/images/python-logo.gif
Downloading http://python.org/images/trans.gif
Downloading http://python.org/images/donate.png
Downloading http://python.org/images/worldmap.jpg
Thread-2 finished downloading images from http://python.org/doc/
 Downloading http://python.org/images/osi-certified-120x100.gif
Thread-2 Starting downloading images from http://python.org/community/
Thread-1 finished downloading images from http://python.org/download/
Thread-1 Starting downloading images from http://python.org/search
Thread-2 finished downloading images from http://python.org/community/
Thread-2 Starting downloading images from http://python.org/about/
Thread-2 finished downloading images from http://python.org/about/
Thread-2 Starting downloading images from http://python.org/news/
Downloading http://python.org/images/Google_Logo_25wht.gif
Thread-1 finished downloading images from http://python.org/search
Thread-1 Starting downloading images from http://python.org
Thread-2 finished downloading images from http://python.org/news/
Thread-2 Starting downloading images from http://python.org/getit/
Downloading http://python.org/images/success/afnic.fr.png
Thread-2 finished downloading images from http://python.org/getit/
```

If you go to the images directory, you will find the downloaded images there.

Summary

A singleton is a design pattern for creating only one instance of a class. Modules in Python are singletons by nature. A classic singleton checks whether the instance was created earlier; if not, it creates and returns it. The Borg singleton uses shared state for all objects. In the example shown in the chapter, we used the Singleton class for accessing a shared resource and a set of URLs to fetch images from, and both threads used it to properly parallelize their work.

In the next chapter, you will learn about other patterns for creating objects, including: factory, the factory method, the abstract factory, and how they help to build objects.

3
Building Factories to Create Objects

In object-oriented development terminology, a factory is a class for creating other objects. Usually this class has methods that accept some parameters and returns some type of object depending on the parameters passed.

In this chapter we will cover:

- How to create a simple factory
- What the Factory Method is, when to use it, and how to implement it for building a tool that can be connected to a variety of web resources
- What the Abstract Factory is, when to use it, and how it is different from the Factory method pattern

So why should we bother ourselves with factories instead of using direct object instantiation?

- Factories provide loose coupling, separating object creation from using specific class implementation.
- A class that uses the created object does not need to know exactly which class is created. All it needs to know is the created class' interface, that is, which created class' methods can be called and with which arguments. Adding new classes is done only in factories as long as the new classes comply with the interface, without modifying the client code.
- The Factory class can reuse existing objects, while direct instantiation always creates a new object.

In the following diagram the Client class uses the Factory class, which has the create_product method. The Client class passes the type of the product to this method and depending on that, the Factory class creates and returns Product1 or Product2.

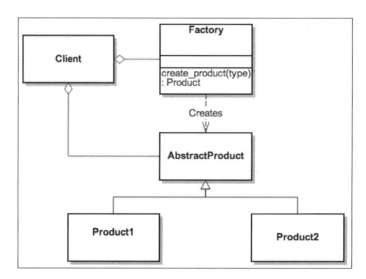

Let's see a simple example of a factory, shown as follows:

```
class SimpleFactory(object):
    @staticmethod # This decorator allows to run method without
              # class instance, .e. SimpleFactory.build_connection
    def build_connection(protocol):
        if protocol == 'http':
          return HTTPConnection()
        elif protocol == 'ftp':
          return FTPConnection()

        else:
          raise RuntimeError('Unknown protocol')

if __name__ == '__main__':
  protocol = raw_input('Which Protocol to use? (http or ftp): ')
  protocol = SimpleFactory.build_connection(protocol)
  protocol.connect()
  print protocol.get_response()
```

In the preceding example, the factory is the SimpleFactory class, which has a static method, build_connection.

You pass it an argument (a type of protocol) and the factory constructs and returns an object depending on the passed argument. So, the client code is not responsible anymore for object creation; it just uses the object generated by the factory without knowing exactly which object was generated as long as the generated object implements some interface.

Factory is not a design pattern by itself; rather, it's a concept that serves as a basis for several design patterns such as Factory Method and Abstract Factory.

The Factory Method

The Factory Method is similar to `SimpleFactory`, but it is a little bit more complicated. As shown in the following diagram, typically this design pattern has an abstract class, `Creator`, that contains the `factory_method` which is responsible for creating some kind of objects. The `some_operation` method then works with the created object. The `ConcreteCreator` class can redefine the `factory_method` to change the created object in the runtime. The `some_operation` method does not care which object is created as long as it implements the `Product` interface and provides the implementation for all methods in that interface.

The essence of this pattern is to define an interface for creating an object, but let the classes that implement the interface decide which class to instantiate. The interface is `factory_method` in the `Creator` and `ConcreteCreator` classes, which decides which subclass of `Product` to create. The Factory Method is based on inheritance; object creation is delegated to the subclasses that implement the `Factory` methods for object creation.

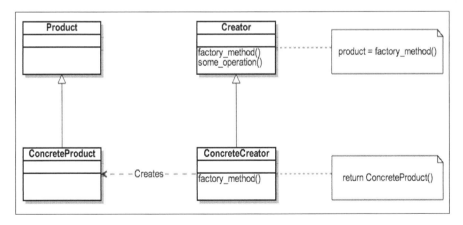

Advantages of using the Factory Method pattern

The main advantages of using the Factory Method pattern are:

- It makes code more universal, not being tied to concrete classes (`ConcreteProduct`) but to interfaces (`Product`) providing low coupling. It separates interfaces from their implementations.

- It decouples the code that creates objects from the code that uses them, reducing the complexity of maintenance. To add a new class, you need to add an additional `else-if` clause.

The Factory Method implementation

In this example we will create a tool for accessing web resources using HTTP or FTP protocol.

Some web resources can be accessed with the FTP protocol. Typically, you open your favorite FTP client, type a URL to connect to, and you can see the directory listing on the server. Choose a file to download.

Some web servers, along with FTP, have HTTP frontend to the same resources. This means that you can open the same web resource with a browser and see the same directory listing as you could see if you opened it with an FTP client.

One of such sites is `ftp.freebsd.org` that can be accessed with `http://ftp.freebsd.org` (HTTP protocol) and `ftp://ftp.freebsd.org` (FTP protocol).

In our application example, we want to be able to get a file list on such servers with FTP and HTTP using the Factory Method pattern.

In this example, we will use one external library called: `BeautifulSoup`, and two libraries from the Python standard library, `urllib2` and `abc`. The `abc` library will be used to implement abstract classes, `urllib2` will be used for making network requests, and `BeautifulSoup` for parsing HTML. If you do not have `BeautifulSoup` installed, run the following command in the terminal:

```
$ sudo pip install beautifulsoup
```

Let's create the `Creator` abstract class that will be named `Connector`. It will be responsible for making the connection to the remote resource (HTTP or FTP), reading the response, and parsing it. This abstract class does not know which port and protocol to use for the connection because the standard port for HTTP is `80` and for FTP is `22`, and the protocol for HTTP is `http` or `https`, and the protocol for FTP is `ftp`. So let's allow the child classes to decide which port to use in the runtime. In the preceding diagram, these two ports will be `ConcreteProducts`.

```python
import abc
import urllib2
from BeautifulSoup import BeautifulStoneSoup

class Connector(object):
  """Abstract class to connect to remote resource."""
  __metaclass__ = abc.ABCMeta # Declares class as abstract class

  def __init__(self, is_secure):
    self.is_secure = is_secure
    self.port = self.port_factory_method()
    self.protocol = self.protocol_factory_method()

  @abc.abstractmethod
  def parse(self):
    """Parses web content.
    This method should be redefined in the runtime."""
    pass

  def read(self, host, path):
    """A generic method for all subclasses, reads web content."""
    url = self.protocol + '://' + host + ':' + str(self.port) + path
    print 'Connecting to ', url
    return urllib2.urlopen(url, timeout=2).read()

  @abc.abstractmethod
  def protocol_factory_method(self):
    """A factory method that must be redefined in subclass."""
    pass
```

```
    @abc.abstractmethod
    def port_factory_method(self):
      """Another factory method that must be redefined in subclass."""
      return FTPPort()
```

So, the `Connector` abstract class provides two Factory Methods to be implemented in the `protocol_factory_method` and `port_factory_method` subclasses. Let's create two concrete creators that will implement these Factory methods:

```
class HTTPConnector(Connector):
    """A concrete creator that creates a HTTP connector and sets in
runtime all its attributes."""
    def protocol_factory_method(self):
      if self.is_secure:
        return 'https'
      return 'http'

    def port_factory_method(self):
      """Here HTTPPort and HTTPSecurePort are concrete objects,
created by factory method."""
      if self.is_secure:
        return HTTPSecurePort()
      return HTTPPort()

    def parse(self, content):
      """Parses web content."""
      filenames = []
      soup = BeautifulStoneSoup(content)
      links = soup.table.findAll('a')
      for link in links:
        filenames.append(link['href'])
      return '\n'.join(filenames)


class FTPConnector(Connector):
    """A concrete creator that creates a FTP connector and sets in
runtime all its attributes."""
    def protocol_factory_method(self):
      return 'ftp'

    def port_factory_method(self):
      return FTPPort()
```

```
def parse(self, content):
  lines = content.split('\n')
  filenames = []
  for line in lines:
    # The FTP format typically has 8 columns, split them
    splitted_line = line.split(None, 8)
    if len(splitted_line) == 9:
      filenames.append(splitted_line[-1])


  return '\n'.join(filenames)
```

Now let's create an interface for our products. The interface consists of one method, namely, __str__ that provides the string representation of the port:

```
class Port(object):
  __metaclass__ = abc.ABCMeta
  """Abstract product. One of its subclasses will be created in
factory methods."""

  @abc.abstractmethod
  def __str__(self):
    pass
```

The three subclasses implementing this interface are HTTPPort, HTTPSecurePort, and FTPPort:

```
class HTTPPort(Port):
  """A concrete product which represents http port."""
  def __str__(self):
    return '80'


class HTTPSecurePort(Port):
  """A concrete product which represents https port."""
  def __str__(self):
    return '443'


class FTPPort(Port):
  """A concrete product which represents ftp port."""
  def __str__(self):
    return '21'
```

And finally, let's create our client code that determines which `Creator` class to instantiate to make a request to the remote resource and print its content:

```
if __name__ == '__main__':
    domain = 'ftp.freebsd.org'
    path = '/pub/FreeBSD/'

    protocol = input('Connecting to {}. Which Protocol to use? (0-http,
1-ftp): '.format(domain))

    if protocol == 0:
        is_secure = bool(input('Use secure connection? (1-yes, 0-no): '))
        connector = HTTPConnector(is_secure)
    else:
        is_secure = False
        connector = FTPConnector(is_secure)

    try:
        content = connector.read(domain, path)
    except urllib2.URLError, e:
        print 'Can not access resource with this method'
    else:
        print connector.parse(content)
```

If you run the preceding script, you will get the following message:

Connecting to ftp.freebsd.org. Which Protocol to use? (0-http, 1-ftp):

You can choose `http` or `ftp` and depending on your decision, the `HTTPConnection` or `FTPConnection` object will be created for making requests and parse the response.

If you choose `http`, you will get the following message:

Use secure connection? (1-yes, 0-no):

If you choose `yes`, `HTTPSecurePort` will be created and if not, `HTTPPort` will be created.

So, the responsibility of making decisions about which port to instantiate was moved to the subclasses of the `Connection` class, decoupling the method that uses the connection (`read`) from the method that creates it (`port_factory_method`).

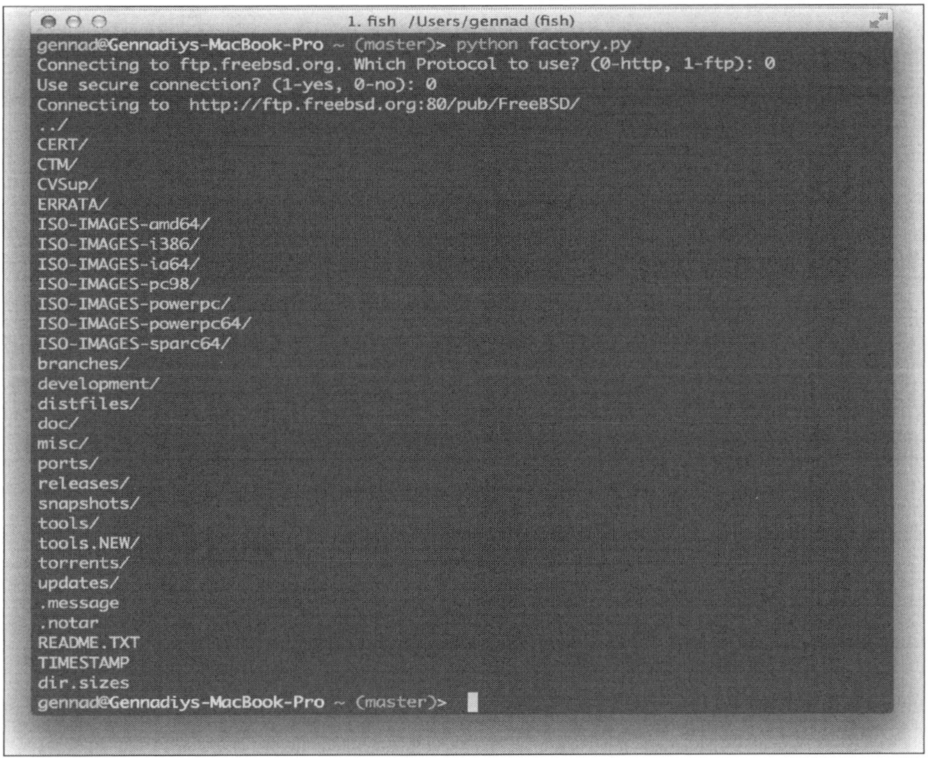

```
● ● ●                    1. fish  /Users/gennad (fish)
gennad@Gennadiys-MacBook-Pro ~ (master)> python factory.py
Connecting to ftp.freebsd.org. Which Protocol to use? (0-http, 1-ftp): 0
Use secure connection? (1-yes, 0-no): 0
Connecting to  http://ftp.freebsd.org:80/pub/FreeBSD/
../
CERT/
CTM/
CVSup/
ERRATA/
ISO-IMAGES-amd64/
ISO-IMAGES-i386/
ISO-IMAGES-ia64/
ISO-IMAGES-pc98/
ISO-IMAGES-powerpc/
ISO-IMAGES-powerpc64/
ISO-IMAGES-sparc64/
branches/
development/
distfiles/
doc/
misc/
ports/
releases/
snapshots/
tools/
tools.NEW/
torrents/
updates/
.message
.notar
README.TXT
TIMESTAMP
dir.sizes
gennad@Gennadiys-MacBook-Pro ~ (master)>
```

Abstract Factory

If the goal of the Factory Method is to move instances creating to subclasses, the goal of an abstract factory is to create families of related objects without depending on their specific classes. As shown in the following diagram, every factory derived from the `AbstractFactory` interface has methods to create instances of two interfaces, `AbstractProduct` and `AnotherAbstractProduct`. The idea is that the created objects should have the same interface, whereas, the created concrete objects are different for every factory. So, if you want to get a different behavior, you can change the factory in runtime and get a full set of different objects.

Abstract Factory is used when you need to create a family of objects that do some work together.

The benefit of using Abstract Factory is that it isolates the creation of objects from the client that needs them, giving the client only the possibility of accessing them through an interface, which makes the manipulation easier. If the products of a family are meant to work together, the `AbstractFactory` class makes it easy to use the objects from only one family at a time. On the other hand, adding new products to the existing factories is difficult because the `AbstractFactory` interface uses a fixed set of products that can be created. This is why adding a new product would mean extending the factory interface, which involves changes in the `AbstractFactory` class and all its subclasses:

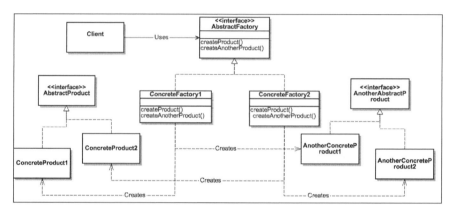

Advantages of using the Abstract Factory pattern

The main advantages of using the Abstract Factory pattern are as follows:

- It simplifies the replacement of product families
- It ensures the compatibility of the products in the product's family
- It isolates the concrete classes from the client

Abstract Factory implementation

The implementation of the preceding example using Abstract Factory is as follows:

```
import abc
import urllib2
from BeautifulSoup import BeautifulStoneSoup
```

The `AbstractFactory` class is used to define the interface of the factories.
Thus, they have the `create_protocol`, `create_port`, and `create_parser` methods.

```
class AbstractFactory(object):
    """Abstract factory interface provides 3 methods to implement in its
    subclasses: create_protocol, create_port and create_parser."""

    __metaclass__ = abc.ABCMeta

    def __init__(self, is_secure):
        """if is_secure is True, factory tries to make connection secure,
otherwise not"""
        self.is_secure = is_secure

    @abc.abstractmethod
    def create_protocol(self):
        pass

    @abc.abstractmethod
    def create_port(self):
        pass

    @abc.abstractmethod
    def create_parser(self):
        pass
```

The `HTTPFactory` class creates its family of related objects: `HTTPPort`,
`HTTPSecurePort`, and `HTTPParser`, whereas, `FTPFactory` creates `FTPPort`
and `FTPParser`.

```
class HTTPFactory(AbstractFactory):
    """Concrete factory for building HTTP connection."""

    def create_protocol(self):
        if self.is_secure:
            return 'https'
        return 'http'

    def create_port(self):
        if self.is_secure:
            return HTTPSecurePort()
        return HTTPPort()

    def create_parser(self):
        return HTTPParser()
```

```
class FTPFactory(AbstractFactory):
    """Concrete factory for building FTP connection."""
    def create_protocol(self):
        return 'ftp'

    def create_port(self):
        return FTPPort()

    def create_parser(self):
        return FTPParser()
```

The following code implements the `Products` classes `Port` and `Parser` with their descendants:

```
class Port(object):
    __metaclass__ = abc.ABCMeta
    """An abstract product, represents port to connect. One of its
subclasses will be created in factory methods."""

    @abc.abstractmethod
    def __str__(self):
        pass

class HTTPPort(Port):
    """A concrete product which represents http port."""
    def __str__(self):
        return '80'

class HTTPSecurePort(Port):
    """A concrete product which represents https port."""
    def __str__(self):
        return '443'

class FTPPort(Port):
    """A concrete product which represents ftp port."""
    def __str__(self):
        return '21'

class Parser(object):
    """An abstract product, represents parser to parse web content.
One of its subclasses will be created in factory methods."""
    __metaclass__ = abc.ABCMeta

    @abc.abstractmethod
    def __call__(self, content):
        pass
```

```
class HTTPParser(Parser):
  def __call__(self, content):
    filenames = []
    soup = BeautifulStoneSoup(content)
    links = soup.table.findAll('a')
    for link in links:
      filenames.append(link.text)
    return '\n'.join(filenames)

class FTPParser(Parser):
  def __call__(self, content):
    lines = content.split('\n')
    filenames = []
    for line in lines:
      splitted_line = line.split(None, 8)
      if len(splitted_line) == 9:
        filenames.append(splitted_line[-1])

    return '\n'.join(filenames)
```

`Connector` is a class that accepts a factory, and this factory is used to inject the components protocol, port, and the method to parse:

```
class Connector(object):
  """A client."""
  def __init__(self, factory):
    """factory is a AbstractFactory instance which creates all
attributes of a connector according to factory class."""
    self.protocol = factory.create_protocol()
    self.port = factory.create_port()
    self.parse = factory.create_parser()

  def read(self, host, path):
    url = self.protocol + '://' + host + ':' + str(self.port) + path
    print 'Connecting to ', url
    return urllib2.urlopen(url, timeout=2).read()

  @abc.abstractmethod
  def parse(self):
    pass
```

In the runtime, the client code determines which factory to use, creates the factory, and instantiates the connector passing the initialized factory.

After that, it calls the `read` method that reads the content of the web resource, parses it, and prints to the stdout:

```python
if __name__ == '__main__':
    domain = 'ftp.freebsd.org'
    path = '/pub/FreeBSD/'

    protocol = input('Connecting to {}. Which Protocol to use? (0-http, 1-ftp): '.format(domain))

    if protocol == 0:
        is_secure = bool(input('Use secure connection? (1-yes, 0-no): '))
        factory = HTTPFactory(is_secure)
    elif protocol == 1:
        is_secure = False
        factory = FTPFactory(is_secure)
    else:
        print 'Sorry, wrong answer'

    connector = Connector(factory)
    try:
        content = connector.read(domain, path)
    except urllib2.URLError, e:
        print 'Can not access resource with this method'
    else:
        print connector.parse(content)
```

Abstract Factory versus Factory Method

Let's look at the instances where we need to use the Abstract Factory or Factory Method.

- Use the Factory Method pattern when there is a need to decouple a client from a particular product it uses. Use the Factory Method to relieve a client of the responsibility of creating and configuring instances of a product.
- Use the Abstract Factory pattern when clients must be decoupled from the product classes. The Abstract Factory pattern can also enforce constraints specifying which classes must be used with others, creating independent families of objects.

Summary

In object-oriented development terminology, a factory is a class for creating other classes. The Factory method defines an interface for creating an object, but lets the classes that implement the interface decide which class to instantiate. The Factory Method makes code more universal, not being tied to concrete classes but to interfaces.

Abstract Factory provides an interface for creating families of related or dependent objects without specifying their concrete classes. It simplifies the replacement of product families and ensures the compatibility of the products consisting in the product family.

In the next chapter you will learn about the Facade pattern, how it simplifies the code for client usage, how it is implemented in the Python source code, and how to implement it yourself.

4

The Facade Design Pattern

Sometimes a subsystem of classes and objects becomes so complex that it's hard to understand how it works. It becomes even more difficult to understand how to use this system and how to decrease the complexity. A Facade design pattern is designed to solve this problem.

In this chapter we will cover:

- The Facade design pattern
- Implementation of the Facade design pattern in Python source code
- Building a weather forecast service in Python

The Facade design pattern

The Facade design pattern provides a unified interface instead of a set of interfaces of some complex subsystem. Facade creates a higher-level interface that simplifies subsystem usage. This design pattern aggregates classes that implement the functionality of the subsystem but does not hide them completely. Facade basically acts as a wrapper. It should not add any new functionality; it should just simplify the access to a system.

Simply put, Facade is an object accumulating a method at a pretty high level of abstraction for working with a complex subsystem. It is important to understand that the client is not deprived of a low-level access to the subsystem classes if he or she wants it, of course. Facade simplifies some operations with the subsystem, but does not impose the use to the client.

In the physical world we always come across Facades; when you turn on the computer, the operating system hides all the internal work of the computer because the OS provides a simplified interface to use the machine.

An automobile is another example: you have a simple interface with steering wheel, gas, and brake pedals but you don't need to know exactly how the engine and the transmission work to drive a car. When you turn a key, the car's electronics sends multiple signals to different parts of the automobile subsystem through a single interface; the ignition key. Facade is known as a structural pattern, as it's used to identify a simple way to realize relationships between entities.

In the following diagram, we have a subsystem consisting of three modules. If the client code will use three modules directly, it will lose flexibility because if one of these three parts will be changed, the client code also needs to be changed. Moreover, the code becomes more complicated to understand and modify. Instead of this, the client uses Facade to aggregate all calls to the subsystem in one function, do_something(). Internally, Facade uses submodules, calls them, and returns some response to the client code. The client code does not need to know anything about these three modules; it can just call the Facade and receive what it wants:

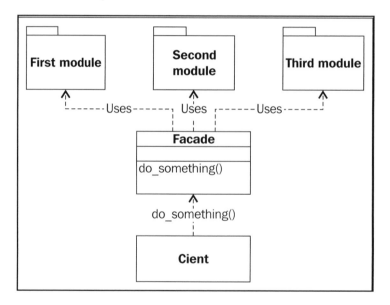

From the architectural point of view, in the design of complex systems we often use the principle of decomposition, in which a complex system is broken down into smaller and simpler subsystems. These subsystems are often developed by different teams of developers. But when they are integrated together and problem of tight coupling arises. If some part of subsystem A changes and subsystem B that uses subsystem A should modify all code that uses the modified code. If we use the Facade, the subsystems can communicate over the Facade and its interface. If Facade's interface remains the same, a code behind the Facade can be modified without affecting the other modules.

Problems solved by the Facade pattern

The problems solved by the Facade pattern are as follows:

- The pattern makes a software library easier to use and test, since the facade has convenient methods for common tasks

- Reduces dependency of using external code, related to the facade code but unrelated to the client code

- Provides a better and clearer API for the client code

Advantages of the Facade design pattern

Let's look at the advantages of the facade design pattern:

- It maintains loose coupling between client and subsystems

- It provides an interface to a set of interfaces in a subsystem (without changing them)

- It wraps a complicated subsystem with a simplier interface

- Subsystem implementation gains flexibility and clients gain simplicity

Facades in Python's standard library

Facades can often be found in Python's source code.

The `isdir` function found in the `os.path` module serves as a Facade outshining work `stat` and `os.stat` modules. Internally `isdir` calls the `os.stat` function and that function in turn calls the `stat()` system call on the given path. This system call returns a structure with members, namely:

- `st_mode`: This indicates some protection bits

- `st_size`: This is the size of the file, in bytes

- `st_atime`: This is the time of the most recent access

`stat.S_ISDIR` internally applies a bit mask `S_IFMT` to detect if the file passed by is actually a directory. This looks pretty confusing, but the good news is that the end user of this function does not need to know these intricacies. The user just needs to know about the `isdir` function.

```
def isdir(s):
    """Return true if the pathname refers to an existing directory."""
    try:
        st = os.stat(s)
    except os.error:
        return False
    return stat.S_ISDIR(st.st_mode)
```

Another example is if you want to load an object that is encoded in a JSON string, you would typically insert the following:

```
import json
json.loads("[1,2,3]")
```

The following code illustrates the implementation of `json.loads`. It has a number of optional parameters, but the only one that is mandatory is the string to decode. So, if no additional parameters are provided, it uses the default decoder implemented as another module in this library and that module in turn uses another `scanner` module to parse the encoded string. So, looks like it is a complex subsystem behind a simple facade:

```
def loads(s, encoding=None, cls=None, object_hook=None, parse_
float=None,
    parse_int=None, parse_constant=None, object_pairs_hook=None,
**kw):
if (cls is None and encoding is None and object_hook is None and
        parse_int is None and parse_float is None and
        parse_constant is None and object_pairs_hook is None and not
kw):
        return _default_decoder.decode(s)
    if cls is None:
        cls = JSONDecoder
    if object_hook is not None:
        kw['object_hook'] = object_hook
    if object_pairs_hook is not None:
        kw['object_pairs_hook'] = object_pairs_hook
    if parse_float is not None:
        kw['parse_float'] = parse_float
    if parse_int is not None:
        kw['parse_int'] = parse_int
    if parse_constant is not None:
        kw['parse_constant'] = parse_constant
    return cls(encoding=encoding, **kw).decode(s)
```

Implementation in Python

Let's write our own example. Imagine that in our application we want to get the current temperature in a city. We had explored a range of available APIs for that and decided to use the `openweathermap.org` resource. It seems like a complicated procedure—a client makes a request to the API, parses it, retrieves necessary data, and converts from Kelvin to Celsius. This increases the complexity of the application. An end user would be happy to call only one method to get the current temperature. So, we can hide all of the intricacies of getting the weather condition behind the facade, providing only one function as the interface for the facade.

Let's build the first component of our complex system. The `WeatherProvider` class is responsible for making requests to the weather API endpoint and returning raw data. In this toy example, we cannot implement this example as a really big and complicated subsystem, so let us assume it is much more complicated than it seems. The `get_weather_data` method takes inputs for city and country, produces a URL string, makes HTTP request, and returns the data received.

```
import urllib
import urllib2
class WeatherProvider(object):
  def __init__(self):
    self.api_url = 'http://api.openweathermap.org/data/2.5/
forecast?q={},{}'
  def get_weather_data(self, city, country):
    city = urllib.quote(city)
    url = self.api_url.format(city, country)
    return urllib2.urlopen(url).read()
```

Next, we need to parse the raw data. The `Parser` class takes raw data and decodes it in the JSON format. The API server sends the data in the following format:

```
{
  "list": [
    {
      "main": {
        "temp": 280.28,

      },
      "dt_txt": "2013-10-24 00:00:00"
    },
    {
      "main": {
        "temp": 279.54,
      },
```

```
      "dt_txt": "2013-10-24 03:00:00"
    },
    {
      "main": {
        "temp": 278.64,
      },
      "dt_txt": "2013-10-26 06:00:00"
    },
    ...
  ]
}
```

So, as you can see, the API gives us the forecast data for every three hours for several days. Since we want to get the forecast only for today, let's collect all temperature information for today and process it later. The method `parse_weather_data`, implemented in the following code, takes a JSON string with weather data. Then it decodes it and starts to iterate over the data. If `start_date` is unassigned (it is the first iteration), we assign it the first day of the forecast that we have. If it is already assigned, we do not reassign a new value but check if we got forecast for the next day. If yes, we just stop the loop, because we need forecast only for today.

```python
from datetime import datetime
import json

class Parser(object):
    def parse_weather_data(self, weather_data):
        parsed = json.loads(weather_data)
        start_date = None
        result = []

        for data in parsed['list']:
            date = datetime.strptime(data['dt_txt'], '%Y-%m-%d %H:%M:%S')
            start_date = start_date or date
            if start_date.day != date.day:
                return result
            result.append(data['main']['temp'])
```

Caching forecast data on the disk to save some traffic seems like a good idea. Let's create a class with methods to save some object to the the hard disk drive and load it from the disk. The `save` method creates a dictionary with two values, including weather information and the time when cache will expire. It lets us know that the cache expires every three hours. The `load` method loads the cached data from the local storage and checks the expiration date. If the forecast object is not expired, the method returns the object. If it is expired, it returns `None`.

```
from datetime import timedelta
import pickle

class Cache(object):
    def __init__(self, filename):
        self.filename = filename

    def save(self, obj):
        with open(self.filename, 'w') as file:
            dct = {
                'obj': obj,
                'expired': datetime.utcnow() + timedelta(hours=3)
            }
            pickle.dump(dct, file)

    def load(self):
        try:
            with open(self.filename) as file:
                result = pickle.load(file)
                if result['expired'] > datetime.utcnow():
                    return result['obj']
        except IOError:
            pass
```

Note that we get data in Kelvin. To convert it to Celsius, we need another part of our subsystem, the converter. The `Converter` class, demonstrated in the following code, has a method that converts Kelvin to Celsius. To do that it subtracts 273.15 from the temperature in Kelvin:

```
class Converter(object):
    def from_kelvin_to_celcius(self, kelvin):
        return kelvin - 273.15
```

And finally the `Weather` class. It receives an iterable of weather forecast for a day and calculates the median forecast:

```
class Weather(object):
    def __init__(self, data):
        result = 0

        for r in data:
            result += r

        self.temperature = result / len(data)
```

So, our system being a toy, has started to become big and monstrous. In the following diagram, the UML diagram of this system is shown:

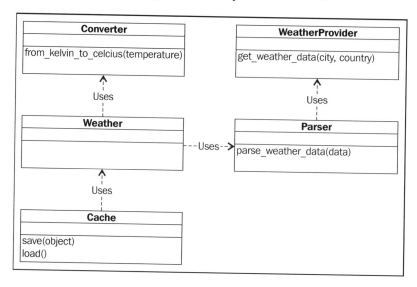

The client will deal with caching, making requests to API, converting, and so on. What if to create a Facade for it? The client will use the get_forecast method, passing it in two strings: the requested city and country, and the method returns the forecasted temperature for today in Celsius.

The following code is of a class of our Facade. In the get_forecast method, first check if we have a cached forecast to return. If yes, return it. Make a request to weather API endpoint, parse response, and create weather instance from the data. Then convert to Celsius, cache it, and return to the client. Much simpler for the client, isn't it?

```
class Facade(object):
  def get_forecast(self, city, country):
    cache = Cache('myfile')

    cache_result = cache.load()

    if cache_result:
      return cache_result
```

```
    else:
      weather_provider = WeatherProvider()
      weather_data = weather_provider.get_weather_data(city, country)

      parser = Parser()
      parsed_data = parser.parse_weather_data(weather_data)

      weather = Weather(parsed_data)
      converter = Converter()
      temperature_celcius = converter.from_kelvin_to_celcius(weather.
  temperature)

      cache.save(temperature_celcius)
      return temperature_celcius
```

Finally, our client code is as follows:

```
if __name__ == '__main__':
  facade = Facade()
  print facade.get_forecast('London', 'UK')
```

Run this code from the command-line prompt and you should receive the following response:

```
$ python facade.py
10.425
```

So the forecast for today is about 10 degrees in London.

Summary

Facades are used when it is needed to provide a simpler interface to a complex subsystem. Facades provide flexibility to subsystem, because all interaction with the client goes through the Facade. It reduces dependency of external library that are used inside the facade, but not related to the client code.

In the next chapter, you will learn about Proxy: another pattern that helps to decrease the complexity of objects interaction and observer: a design pattern to broadcast some information to multiple receivers whose amount can be changed in the runtime.

5

Facilitating Object Communication with Proxy and Observer Patterns

Sometimes you need to work with a large object — so large that it is better to defer its creation to the moment when it is actually used to save some memory and time. When it is created, it is better not to create it again on every new request, but use the previously created object and create a new reference. When all parts of the code have completed work with it, it is required that some memory be freed up as soon as possible. It means we need to count references to the heavy object, and to implement it, we need a middleman that does all this intermediate work. A proxy is the solution to this problem.

A Proxy is a design pattern that helps to decouple the client code from the object that the client code uses. It means that the client code will use a surrogate proxy object that acts like a real object; however, the surrogate object will delegate all calls to the real object.

The example described previously is known as **lazy initialization**. You defer the object initialization until you really need it. But it is not the only one use-case of a proxy. Proxies help to implement logging, facilitate network connections, control access to shared objects, implement reference counting, and have many other uses.

Proxy design pattern

A proxy is a class, functioning as an interface to another class that has the same interface as the proxy. The client code instantiates and works directly with the proxy, whereas, the proxy contains the real-object instance and delegates all calls to it, adding the proxy's own logic.

The proxy serves as an interface with many things: a network connection, a large object in memory, a file, or some other resource that is expensive or impossible to duplicate.

In the following diagram, **Proxy** and **RealSubject** are inherited from the same interface—**Subject**. **Client** uses **Proxy** which delegates calls to **RealSubject**.

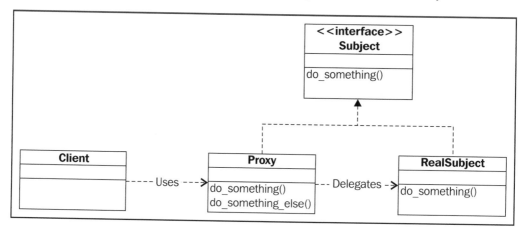

Problems solved by the Proxy pattern

The Proxy pattern solves the following problems that arise if objects maintain tight coupling:

- The Proxy provides a placeholder for another object to control access to it
- The Proxy uses an extra level of indirection to support distributed, controlled, or intelligent access
- The Proxy adds a wrapper and delegation to protect the real component from undue complexity

The use of the Proxy pattern

The Proxy pattern can be typically used when you need to extend another object's functionalities, specifically the following:

- To control access to another object, for example, for security reasons.
- To log all calls to **Subject** with its parameters.
- To connect to **Subject**, which is located on remote machine or another address space. A **Proxy** has an interface of a remote object but also handles the connection routine that is transparent to the caller.
- To instantiate a heavy object only when it is really needed. It can also cache a heavy object (or part of it).
- To temporarily store some calculation results before returning to multiple clients that can share these results.
- To count references to an object.

Advantages and disadvantages of the Proxy design pattern

The main pros and cons of proxy are as follows:

- A proxy can optimize the performance of an application, using caching of heavy or frequently used objects.
- A proxy allows to improve the security of an application, checking access rights in **Proxy** and delegating to **RealSubject** only if the rights are sufficient.
- Facilitating interaction between remote systems, a proxy can take over the job of network connections and transmission routine, delegating calls to remote objects.
- Sometimes use of the Proxy pattern can increase the response time from the object. For example, if you use proxy for lazy initialization and the object is requested for the first time, the time of the response will be increased by initialization time.

Implementation in Python

In this example, we need to instantiate a huge object, `RealSubject`, which contains 10 million digits. Instantiating it takes some time and space in RAM; that's why we create a proxy to interface it.

In the following example, we will import the meta class ABCMeta and the abstractmethod decorator. We will use them to implement abstract classes. An abstract class is a class that has methods with no implementation. The abstract class cannot be instantiated, and its descendants also cannot be instantiated unless they provide implementation for methods marked by the abstractmethod decorator. Thus, if you want to implement abstract class, assign its __metaclass__ attribute to ABCMeta and decorate the methods having no implementation with abstractmethod decorator.

First, let's create an abstract class that provides an interface for both RealSubject and its proxy:

```
from abc import ABCMeta, abstractmethod
import random

class AbstractSubject(object):
    """A common interface for the real and proxy objects."""

    __metaclass__ = ABCMeta

    @abstractmethod
    def sort(self, reverse=False):
        pass
```

Next is the RealSubject class, which inherits the AbstractSubject abstract class, implementing the sort method.

```
class RealSubject(AbstractSubject):
    """A class for a heavy object which takes a lot of memory
        space and takes some time to instantiate."""

    def __init__(self):
        self.digits = []

        for i in xrange(10000000):
            self.digits.append(random.random())

    def sort(self, reverse=False):
        self.digits.sort()

        if reverse:
            self.digits.reverse()
```

A `Proxy` class (instead of `RealSubject`) will be instantiated by the client code. The proxy contains the count of references to the `RealSubject` class and keeps the only instance of `RealSubject`, creating it only if it has not been created before. If it has been created, the `Proxy` class increments reference count and returns a new link to the `RealSubject` class.

The next interesting point is in the `sort` method. It logs the arguments of the method and calls the method of `RealSubject`.

Finally, in the destructor, the reference count is decreased on every deletion of the reference to `RealSubject` and if no references are left, the object is marked to be garbage collected.

```
class Proxy(AbstractSubject):
    """A proxy which has the same interface as RealSubject."""

    reference_count = 0

    def __init__(self):
        """A constructor which creates an object if it is not exist and
            caches it otherwise."""

        if not getattr(self.__class__, 'cached_object', None):
            self.__class__.cached_object = RealSubject()
            print 'Created new object'
        else:
            print 'Using cached object'

        self.__class__.reference_count += 1

        print 'Count of references = ', self.__class__.reference_count

    def sort(self, reverse=False):
        """The args are logged by the Proxy."""

        print 'Called sort method with args:'
        print locals().items()

        self.__class__.cached_object.sort(reverse=reverse)

    def __del__(self):
```

```
"""Decreases a reference to an object, if the number of
   references is 0, delete the object."""
self.__class__.reference_count -= 1

if self.__class__.reference_count == 0:
  print 'Number of reference_count is 0. Deleting cached
     object...'
  del self.__class__.cached_object

print 'Deleted object. Count of objects = ',
   self.__class__.reference_count
```

In the following client code, we create three instances of the `Proxy` class. While creating the first instance, the `RealSubject` object will be created and stored in `Proxy.cached_object`. The next two instances of `Proxy` will reuse the previously created `RealSubject` object. Besides that, `Proxy` keeps number of links to the `RealSubject`.

Then we run the `sort` method of the proxy. The proxy logs parameters and delegates this call to `RealSubject`.

Finally we delete the second link to the `RealSubject` object, confirming that the reference count works as expected.

```
if __name__ == '__main__':
  proxy1 = Proxy()
  print

  proxy2 = Proxy()
  print
  proxy3 = Proxy()
  print

  proxy1.sort(reverse=True)
  print

  print 'Deleting proxy2'
  del proxy2
  print

  print 'The other objects are deleted upon program termination'
```

The result of program execution will appear, as shown in the following screenshot:

Observer design pattern

The Observer design pattern tries to facilitate one-to-many relationships in software engineering. There are many situations that deal with one-to-many relationships: several readers subscribe to a blog, several event listeners subscribe to handle mouse clicks on a user interface item, or several phone applications subscribe to receive a notification when they get data from the Internet.

The Observer design pattern is very similar to subscribing to a newspaper in the following aspects:

- The subscriber opens subscription for the newspaper
- You subscribe to the newspaper
- Somebody else subscribes to the newspaper
- When there's a new newspaper, you and that somebody else get a new newspaper
- If you don't want to receive the newspaper anymore, you cancel your subscription and you will not receive next newspaper (but others will)

This is a kind of publishing-subscriber pattern, and in software engineering, unlike the newspaper, it uses any kind of information, such as new data received from some other resources, a concurrent thread signal, or a signal from an operational system. This information should be delivered to subscribers and the Observer design pattern serves for managing subscription and delivering it.

In the Observer pattern, an object called the subject keeps a set of other objects called observers, and in case there are any state changes, it notifies them by calling one of their methods.

As shown in the following diagram, **Observer** is an interface that has the abstract method `notify`. **ConcreteObserverA** and **ConcreteObserverB** are derived from the abstract **Observer** interface and need to implement the abstract method `notify`. A subject keeps a set of instances of concrete observers, adds new **Observer** instances calling `register_observer`, and removes instances calling the `unregister_observer` method. When some event happens, the **Subject** interface calls the `notify_observers` method. In this method, each registered observer is called with the `notify` method.

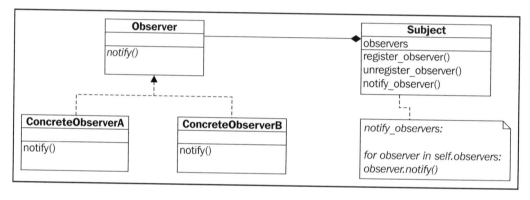

Subject is the static part of the system; throughout the application lifetime, there is only one **Subject**. On the contrary, **Observers** are the variable part. There can be many or even zero observers, and this value changes during the lifetime of the application. All the parts that are updated often are typically implemented as **Observers**.

Problems solved by the Observer pattern

If there is a requirement that a particular object change its state, and depending on these changes some or a group of objects automatically change their state, we need to implement the Observer pattern to reduce the coupling between objects.

A real-world example can be found on microblogging services, such as Twitter; when you post a new tweet (change the state of you feed), all your followers (observers) will be notified—their timeline will be updated with your new tweet.

Use of the Observer pattern

The Observer pattern is used when a change in one object leads to a change in other objects, and you don't know how many objects should be changed.

Advantages of the Observer pattern

The Observer design pattern has the following advantages:

- Maintaining a loose coupling between **Subject** and **Observers**. The **Subject** only knows the list of **Observers** and their interfaces; it doesn't care about its concrete class, details of implementation, and so on.
- Ability of broadcast messaging between **Subject** and **Observers**.
- The number of **Observers** can be changed at runtime.
- The **Subject** can keep any number of **Observers**.

Implementation in Python

Now we'll create a simple subject that will be able to add, remove, and notify the observers. In this simplified example, the `notify` method of every observer will get a Unix timestamp and will print it out in either the USA format (12 hour) or the EU (24 hour) format.

Let's create `Subject`, which will keep a list of observers in `self.observers` and provide methods to add and remove observers with `register_observer` and `unregister_observer`. When we want to send some information to all observers, we simply call the `notify_observers` method, which passes a new value of the Unix timestamp to the observers.

```python
import time

class Subject(object):
def __init__(self):
  self.observers = []
  self.cur_time = None


def register_observer(self, observer):
  if observer in self.observers:
    print observer, 'already in subscribed observers'
  else:
```

```
        self.observers.append(observer)

    def unregister_observer(self, observer):
      try:
        self.observers.remove(observer)
      except ValueError:
        print 'No such observer in subject'

    def notify_observers(self):
      self.cur_time = time.time()
      for observer in self.observers:
        observer.notify(self.cur_time)
```

Now we create an abstract class for the observer, with only one method, `notify`, which `Subject` will call in its `notify_observers` method. We will use the same abstractmethod decorator described in the previous chapter to implement the abstract method `notify`.

```
from abc import ABCMeta, abstractmethod
import datetime


class Observer(object):
    """Abstract class for observers, provides notify method as
       interface for subjects."""

    __metaclass__ = ABCMeta

    @abstractmethod
    def notify(self, unix_timestamp):
      pass
```

And a couple of concrete observer derived from abstract observer. They need to implement notify method. This method will take UNIX timestamp converts it to 12H or 24H format and print it to standard out.

```
class USATimeObserver(Observer):
    def __init__(self, name):
      self.name = name

    def notify(self, unix_timestamp):
```

```
    time =
datetime.datetime.fromtimestamp(int(unix_timestamp)).strftime('%Y-
%m-%d %I:%M:%S%p')
    print 'Observer', self.name, 'says:', time


class EUTimeObserver(Observer):
  def __init__(self, name):
    self.name = name

  def notify(self, unix_timestamp):
    time =
datetime.datetime.fromtimestamp(int(unix_timestamp)).strftime('%Y-
%m-%d %H:%M:%S')
    print 'Observer', self.name, 'says:', time
```

The following is the starting point of the application. Initially, we create a first observer, register it in `subject`, and send some information to this sole observer. The observer prints the current date in the 12-hour format. Next, we create a second observer, register, and send information to both the observers.

They print the current date in the 12-hour format and the 24-hour format. After that we unregister the first observer and send information only to the second observer. It prints the current date in the 24-hour format.

```
  if __name__ == '__main__':
    subject = Subject()

    print 'Adding usa_time_observer'
    observer1 = USATimeObserver('usa_time_observer')
    subject.register_observer(observer1)
    subject.notify_observers()

    time.sleep(2)
    print 'Adding eu_time_observer'
    observer2 = EUTimeObserver('eu_time_observer')
    subject.register_observer(observer2)
    subject.notify_observers()

    time.sleep(2)
    print 'Removing usa_time_observer'
    subject.unregister_observer(observer1)
    subject.notify_observers()
```

If you run the application, you should get results similar to what's shown in the
following screenshot:

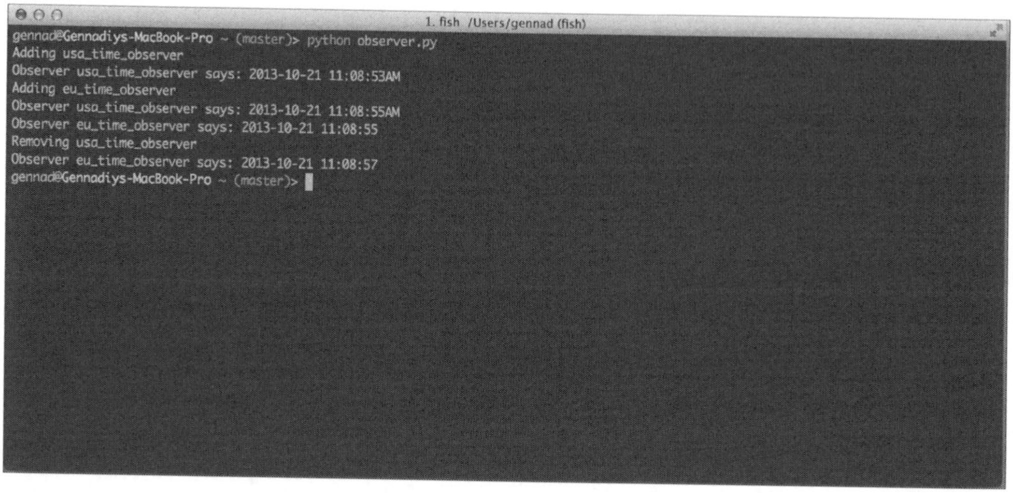

In the previous example, we explicitly passed the `unix_timestamp` from the subject
to the concrete observers. The other frequent use is to pass the **Subject** instance itself
instead of data. In that case, the previous example would be written as follows:

```
def notify_observers(self):
    self.cur_time = time.time()
    for observer in self.observers:
        observer.notify(self)
```

Observer would to get the necessary data from the subject itself, by calling the
subject's methods and accessing attributes. The other option is not to pass any data
at all. The observer will be notified that some event happened and that it will be
responsible for getting the updated value and interpreting as it wants.

Summary

A proxy is a class, functioning as an interface to another class, which has the same interface as the proxy. The client code instantiates and works directly with the proxy, whereas, the proxy delegates actual work to a client class. Proxies have many uses, particularly for caching, reference count, and access-right control. Users of proxy should be careful to avoid an increase in response time. The Observer design pattern is used when you need to implement one-to-many relationships, for instance, to broadcast the same information to multiple listeners called observers. The Observer design pattern maintains loose coupling between the subject and observers because the only thing the subject knows about the observers is the interface, namely, which method to call to notify it. The number of observers can be arbitrary and changed in the runtime.

In the next chapter you will learn about the Command design pattern, how it is used to encapsulate the call in one object, and how to implement the undo functionality, history, and macros with it.

6

Encapsulating Calls with the Command Pattern

In this chapter you will learn about the Command design pattern, how to implement undo and macro operations, and write very simple Unix command variations, which can be cancelled after execution.

Imagine that you are writing the printer program and want to implement the printer spooler. What is the the easiest way to do it? Create a `Spooler` class with methods to add and remove printer jobs. The easiest way to execute printer jobs is to create an object, which contains all necessary information: text to print, number of copies, color, quality, and so on. The spooler will need to call the `execute` method of the print job, and the print job will take care of everything by itself.

That's how the Command Pattern works: you create an object, which represents and encapsulates all the information needed to call a method at a later time. This information includes the method name, the object that owns the method, and values for the method parameters.

You are able to pass these command objects to any code that knows how to call its `execute` method, save these objects, and return from methods as any other object. For instance, in *Chapter 5, Facilitating Object Communication with Proxy and Observer Patterns*, you learned about the Observer pattern, whose main job was notifying objects about some event. With the Command Pattern, you are able to pass the Command instance as an observer and when the Subject notifies the observers about some event, the Command instance will be called and some work encapsulated in it will be done.

Command Pattern terminology

To understand how the Command Pattern works, let's define some terminologies:

- **Command**: This is an interface for executing an operation.
- **ConcreteCommand**: This class extends the **Command** interface and implements the `execute` method. This class creates a binding between the action and the receiver.
- **Client**: This class creates the `ConcreteCommand` class and associates it with the receiver.
- **Invoker**: This class asks the command to carry out the request.
- **Receiver**: This class knows how to perform the operation.

In the following diagram, the `Invoker` class calls the `execute` method of an object with the Command interface. Actually, it is an object of the `ConcreteCommand` class, in which the `execute` method calls an object of the `Receiver` class that does some actual work.

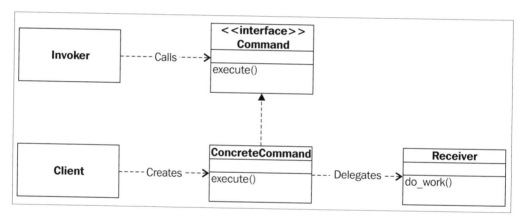

The Command design pattern provides an interface to call a method to perform some job and encapsulates all necessary information to do it in one object call, which can be run separately after instantiation.

Use cases of the Command design pattern

It is better to apply the command in the following cases:

- When you need to keep a history of requests. An invoker can save command instances after calling its `execute` method to implement history functionality somewhere.

- When you need to implement callback functionality. If you pass to the invoker two objects one after another, the second object will be a callback for the first.

- When you need requests to be handled at variant times or in variant orders. To achieve this, you can pass the command objects to different invokers, which are invoked by different conditions.

- When the invoker should be decoupled from the object handling the invocation.

- When you need to implement the undo functionality. To achieve this, you need to define a method that cancels a operation performed in the `execute` method. For example, if you created a file, you need to delete it.

Advantages and disadvantages of the Command design pattern

The pros and cons of the Command design pattern are as follows:

- It is useful when creating a structure, particulary when the creating of a request and executing are not dependent on each other. It means that the **Command** instance can be instantiated by **Client**, but run sometime later by the **Invoker**, and the **Client** and **Invoker** may not know anything about each other.

- This pattern helps in terms of extensibility as we can add a new command without changing the existing code.

- It allows you to create a sequence of commands named macro. To run the macro, create a list of **Command** instances and call the `execute` method of all commands.

The main disadvantage of the Command Pattern is the increase in the number of classes for each individual command.

Implementation in Python

For this example, we will create an extremely simple implementation of several Unix commands: ls, touch, and rm. We are going to use them in our shell, which we will write sometime later. The killer feature of the shell will be the possibility to undo all the operations executed since the shell started. Let's use the Command design pattern to do it.

In this example, we will use the abc module that provides the abstractmethod decorator to make methods abstract, so that this method should be implemented in derived classes to instantiate them. Also, we need to assign abc.ABCMeta to the __metaclass__ class attribute to let the abstractmethod decorator work. More information can be found in Python's standard library documentation at http://docs.python.org/2/library/abc.html.

First, let's create an interface for our commands as shown in the following code:

```python
import abc
import os

history = []

class Command(object):
    """The command interface."""

    __metaclass__ = abc.ABCMeta

    @abc.abstractmethod
    def execute(self):
        """Method to execute the command."""
        pass

    @abc.abstractmethod
    def undo(self):
        """A method to undo the command."""
        pass
```

Every command can be executed and undone. The first command will be ls, which lists the current directory content.

```python
class LsCommand(Command):
    """Concrete command that emulates ls unix command behavior."""

    def __init__(self, receiver):
```

```
    self.receiver = receiver

def execute(self):
  """The command delegates the call to its receiver."""
  self.receiver.show_current_dir()

def undo(self):
  """Can not undo ls command."""
  pass
```

So, the `ls` command does not have any logic; it just contains the receiver and delegates the actual work to the receiver. Let's create the receiver for it with the following code:

```
class LsReceiver(object):
  def show_current_dir(self):
    """The receiver knows how to execute the command."""

    cur_dir = './'

    filenames = []
    for filename in os.listdir(cur_dir):
      if os.path.isfile(os.path.join(cur_dir, filename)):
        filenames.append(filename)

    print 'Content of dir: ', ' '.os.path.join(filenames)
```

The Unix `touch` command generally creates a file if it does not exist and updates the access time of the file if it is already created. In our example, we will implement it using the `os.utime` function, whose effect is similar to running the Unix `touch` command. Thus, we will have the `TouchCommand` class derived from the **Command** interface that has the `execute` method, and unlike the `ls` command, it will also have an `undo` method implemented. The `touch` command creates a file and to undo the command, we need to delete it.

To do the work, `TouchCommand` delegates all calls to `TouchReceiver` that has the `create_file` and `delete_file` methods, which literally create and delete file.

```
class TouchCommand(Command):
  """Concrete command that emulates touch unix command
    behavior."""

  def __init__(self, receiver):
    self.receiver = receiver
  def execute(self):
    self.receiver.create_file()

  def undo(self):
```

```
        self.receiver.delete_file()

    class TouchReceiver(object):

        def __init__(self, filename):
            self.filename = filename

        def create_file(self):
            """Actual implementation of unix touch command."""
            with file(self.filename, 'a'):
                os.utime(self.filename, None)

        def delete_file(self):
            """Undo unix touch command. Here we simply delete the file."""
            os.remove(self.filename)
```

It's not so easy to implement an undo operation for the rm command, which removes a file. To achieve this, we will not delete file; we'll just mimic a deletion by renaming it.

```
    class RmCommand(Command):
        """Concrete command that emulates rm unix command behavior."""
        def __init__(self, receiver):
            self.receiver = receiver

        def execute(self):
            self.receiver.delete_file()

        def undo(self):
            self.receiver.undo()

    class RmReceiver(object):

        def __init__(self, filename):
            self.filename = filename
            self.backup_name = None

        def delete_file(self):
            """Deletes file with creating backup to restore it in undo
               method."""
            self.backup_name = '.' + self.filename
            os.rename(self.filename, self.backup_name)

        def undo(self):
            """Restores the deleted file."""
            original_name = self.backup_name[1:]
            os.rename(self.backup_name, original_name)
            self.backup_name = None
```

That's our invoker. It takes a list of commands to create and delete files. When we create or delete a file, all these commands are executed one after the other.

It is noteworthy that the invoker maintains a history of executed commands. We need it to implement undo operations. When we want to undo the commands, we get a list of executed commands. And at the end of it, the invoker calls the undo method of all the previously executed commands.

```python
class Invoker(object):
    def __init__(self, create_file_commands, delete_file_commands):
        self.create_file_commands = create_file_commands
        self.delete_file_commands = delete_file_commands
        self.history = []

    def create_file(self):
        print 'Creating file...'

        for command in self.create_file_commands:
            command.execute()
            self.history.append(command)

        print 'File created.\n'

    def delete_file(self):
        print 'Deleting file...'
        for command in self.delete_file_commands:
            command.execute()
            self.history.append(command)
        print 'File deleted.\n'

    def undo_all(self):
        print 'Undo all...'

        for command in reversed(self.history):
            command.undo()

        print 'Undo all finished.'
```

And the last part is our client code, which creates command objects, assigns them receivers, and passes these commands to the receiver.

```python
if __name__ == '__main__':
    # Client
```

```
# List files in current directory
ls_receiver = LsReceiver()
ls_command = LsCommand(ls_receiver)

# Create a file
touch_receiver = TouchReceiver('test_file')
touch_command = TouchCommand(touch_receiver)

# Delete created file
rm_receiver = RmReceiver('test_file')
rm_command = RmCommand(rm_receiver)

create_file_commands = [ls_command, touch_command, ls_command]
delete_file_commands = [ls_command, rm_command, ls_command]

invoker = Invoker(create_file_commands, delete_file_commands)

invoker.create_file()
invoker.delete_file()
invoker.undo_all()
```

If you run the script, you will get the message as shown in the following screenshot:

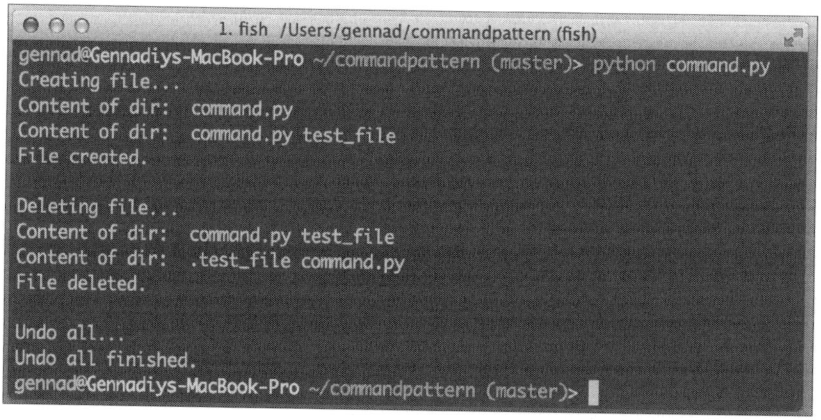

The script created a new file, test_file, as a result of the invoker.create_file() invocation.

Then, the invocation of delete_file() renamed test_file to .test_file, emulating the backup functionality.

Finally, the undo_all invocation annuls all executed commands, executing the corresponding undo method of every executed command and leaves us with the same directory content we had before running the script.

Summary

The Command design pattern provides an interface to call a method to perform some job and encapsulates all necessary information to do it in one object call, which can be run separately and later after instantiation.

The Command design pattern can be used to achieve undo operations if you implement a method that cancels the execute function result.

The Command design pattern can be used to implement the history of executed operations and macros as a set of Command instances, which can be executed in a sequence.

In the next chapter, you will learn about the Template Method pattern that helps you to adjust an algorithm to different contexts with minimal changes.

7
Redefining Algorithms with the Template Method

Sometimes you have one algorithm that needs to be changed with slight modifications. For example, imagine you are building authentication for some website where you should be able to authenticate users via social network accounts. The authentication processes via Twitter and Facebook, for example, are similar in general but still require some changes; they use different URLs and pass different data. Naively, you implement this algorithm again and again from start to finish, but someday you realize that there are obvious code duplication and difficulties with code maintenance; to change the logic of an algorithm, you need to change your code at several places for every implementation.

But, apart from the naive version, we have a dedicated pattern to handle such tasks: a Template Method design pattern.

The Template Method design pattern

The main idea of Template Method is to create a method that will hold a sequence of steps (primitive operations) for our algorithm to achieve some goal. These primitive operations will be implemented in separate methods. Some methods are the same for every kind of algorithm and some methods are different. The same methods will be implemented in the abstract class, whereas, the implementation of different methods will be in separate classes for every kind of algorithm.

So, the sequence of steps to implement the Template Method is as follows:

1. Create a method for the algorithm.
2. Split the algorithm's implementation into several methods.
3. Methods that are the same for every class should be implemented in the base class, whereas, specific methods should be implemented in the inherited class.

In the following diagram, **AbstractClass** has a method `template_method` that consists of calls to `primitive_operation1` and `primitive_operation2` methods. These two methods provide the default implementation of the algorithm in `template_method`. In the **ConcreteClass**, `primitive_operation2` is redefined, leaving `primitive_operation1` as it is. The redefined `primitivie_operation2` redefines some part of the algorithm in `template_method`.

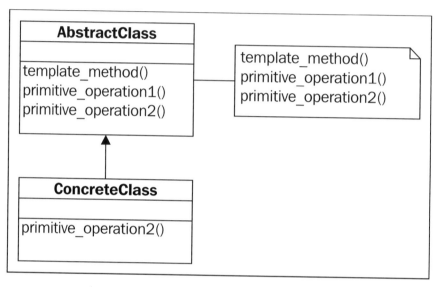

The benefits of the Template Method design pattern

The main benefit of the Template Method design pattern is that it allows a class to control and expose its parts, providing good extensibility. In addition to this, it provides the following benefits:

- Minimizes code duplication—no need to write similar code again and again
- The algorithm itself is located in one place of code, so there is no need to change it in different parts
- Ease of code modification; you need to create a new class and implement some methods instead of rewriting the whole algorithm

Using hooks

The hook is a method that can be defined in an abstract class and can be overridden in concrete classes. The difference between primitive operations and hooks is that hooks can be overridden by a derived class but is not obligated to do it, whereas, a primitive operation must be implemented or the program will raise `NotImplementedError` during the execution. Hooks are used for small changes in an algorithm while avoiding code duplication.

Implementation in Python

Imagine you are building a news aggregator and want to get the latest news from a lot of news sites. The news sites typically provide news with RSS and Atom protocols. These protocols are based on XML and are mostly similar with exception to some details.

The following is an example of an RSS feed. Here we have a set of item tags that correspond to a published item (news, or blog posts, and so on).

In every item, we have a short title, longer description, and a direct link to an item as shown in the following code:

```xml
<?xml version="1.0" encoding="ISO-8859-1" ?>
  <rss version="2.0">
    <channel>
      <title>A RSS example</title>
      <link>http://example.com</link>
      <description>Description of RSS example</description>
      <item>
        <title>The first news</title>
        <link>http://example.com/first</link>
        <description>Some description of the first
          news</description>
      </item>
      <item>
        <guid>urn:uuid:1225c695-cfb8-4ebb-aaaa-80da344efa6a</id>
        <title>The second news</title>
        <link>example.com/second</link>
        <description>Some description of the second
          news</description>
        <pubDate>Wed, 30 Sep 2013 13:00:00 GMT</pubDate>
      </item>
    </channel>
  </rss>
```

An Atom feed is similar, but it has some differences. The following is the same example represented in the Atom format:

```
<?xml version="1.0" encoding="utf-8"?>
<feed xmlns="http://www.w3.org/2005/Atom">
<title>A RSS example</title>
<subtitle>Description of RSS example</subtitle>
<link href="http://example.org/"/>
<entry>
  <id>urn:uuid:1225c695-cfb8-4ebb-aaaa-80da344efa6a</id>
  <title>The first news</title>
  <link href="http://example.com/first"/>
  <summary>Some description of the second news</summary>
  <updated>2013-09-30T13:00:00Z</updated>
</entry>
</feed>
```

As we see, Atom uses the `<entry>` tag instead of the `<item>` tag, and the link is stored in an attribute instead of a text node. Also, Atom uses the `<summary>` tag instead of `<description>`, and it uses `<update>` instead of `<pubDate>`. Additionally, every feed provider can use their own version of the `<guid>`/`<id>` format, or this item can even be omitted.

We need to use different algorithms to parse the feeds, but everything else should be the same for both the feeds; we make a request, get a response, and print the parsed content for the user.

We will use the Google News public feed that provides news in an Atom format, and the Yahoo! News public feed that provides feeds in RSS. Say, our client wants to get the latest news printed to `stdout`, without the knowledge of the type of feed. To do this, let's decide with our parsing algorithm:

1. Get a URL to make a request to the feed server.
2. Get the raw content.
3. Parse it.
4. Print it for the end user.

How can we ensure that steps 2 and 4 will be the same for all the feeds, whereas 1 and 3 will be special?

To do this, let's create an abstract class that will hold our algorithm in the `print_top_news` method.

We need to import `minidom` from `xml.dom`.

```python
import urllib2    # To make http requests to RSS and Atom feeds

class AbstractNewsParser(object):
  def __init__(self):
    # Prohibit creating class instance
    if self.__class__ is AbstractNewsParser:
      raise TypeError('abstract class cannot be instantiated')

  def print_top_news(self):
    """A Template method. Returns 3 latest news for every news
      website."""
    url = self.get_url()
    raw_content = self.get_raw_content(url)
    content = self.parse_content(raw_content)

    cropped = self.crop(content)

    for item in cropped:
      print 'Title: ', item['title']
      print 'Content: ', item['content']
      print 'Link: ', item['link']
      print 'Published: ', item['published']
      print 'Id: ', item['id']

  def get_url(self):
    raise NotImplementedError()

  def get_raw_content(self, url):
    return urllib2.urlopen(url).read()

  def parse_content(self, content):
    raise NotImplementedError()

  def crop(self, parsed_content, max_items=3):
    return parsed_content[:max_items]
```

In the preceding code, we left `get_raw_content` and `parse_content` as not implemented to let subclasses implement them. We cannot provide the implementation because every concrete feed parser will have its own method to parse and a method that returns the URL for making requests. In the `parse_content` method, we parse the XML and assign all of the parsed values to a dictionary, which has the same format for Atom and RSS.

The following is the `YahooParser` class, which is inherited from the `AbstractNewsParser` abstract class and provides implementation for the `get_url` and `parse_content` abstract methods. The `parse_content` method parses RSS feed and returns a dictionary filled with parsed data.

```
class YahooParser(AbstractNewsParser):
  def get_url(self):
    return 'http://news.yahoo.com/rss/'

  def parse_content(self, raw_content):

    parsed_content = []

    dom = minidom.parseString(raw_content)

    for node in dom.getElementsByTagName('item'):

      parsed_item = {}

      try:
        parsed_item['title'] =
          node.getElementsByTagName('title')[0].childNodes[0].
            nodeValue
      except IndexError:
        parsed_item['title'] = None

      try:
        parsed_item['content'] =
          node.getElementsByTagName('description')[0].childNodes[0].
            nodeValue
      except IndexError:
        parsed_item['content'] = None

      try:
        parsed_item['link'] =
          node.getElementsByTagName('link')[0].childNodes[0].nodeValue
      except IndexError:
        parsed_item['link'] = None
```

```
try:
  parsed_item['id'] =
    node.getElementsByTagName('guid')[0].childNodes[0].nodeValue
except IndexError:
  parsed_item['id'] = None


try:
  parsed_item['published'] =
    node.getElementsByTagName('pubDate')[0].childNodes[0].
      nodeValue
except IndexError:
  parsed_item['published'] = None


parsed_content.append(parsed_item)


return parsed_content
```

The same is for `GoogleParser`; we parse an Atom feed and assign parsed values to a dictionary as follows:

```
class GoogleParser(AbstractNewsParser):
  def get_url(self):
    return 'https://news.google.com/news/feeds?output=atom'


  def parse_content(self, raw_content):
    parsed_content = []
    dom = minidom.parseString(raw_content)

    for node in dom.getElementsByTagName('entry'):

      parsed_item = {}

      try:
        parsed_item['title'] =
          node.getElementsByTagName('title')[0].childNodes[0].
            nodeValue
      except IndexError:
        parsed_item['title'] = None

      try:
```

```
          parsed_item['content'] =
            node.getElementsByTagName('content')[0].childNodes[0].
              nodeValue
        except IndexError:
          parsed_item['content'] = None

        try:
          parsed_item['link'] =
            node.getElementsByTagName('link')[0].getAttribute('href')
        except IndexError:
          parsed_item['link'] = None

        try:
          parsed_item['id'] =
            node.getElementsByTagName('id')[0].childNodes[0].nodeValue
        except IndexError:
          parsed_item['id'] = None

        try:
          parsed_item['published'] =
            node.getElementsByTagName('updated')[0].childNodes[0].
              nodeValue
        except IndexError:
          parsed_item['published'] = None

        parsed_content.append(parsed_item)

    return parsed_content
```

In our client code, we create instances of RSS and Atom parsers and print out the news in the `print_top_news()` template method indicating that they have parsed, as illustrated in the following code. Both the parsers use the algorithm defined in `print_top_news()`, but the implementation of the algorithm differs because we have redefined several steps of the algorithm using the Template Method pattern.

```
if __name__ == '__main__':
  google = GoogleParser()
  yahoo = YahooParser()

  print 'Google: \n', google.print_top_news()
  print 'Yahoo: \n', yahoo.print_top_news()
```

Summary

The Template Method is a design pattern that defines the basis of an algorithm and enables successors to redefine some steps of the algorithm without changing its structure. The Template Method pattern allows good extensibility of the algorithm, but only where permitted. This design pattern is well applied when you have an algorithm whose behavior is common but the implementation may vary and you have some steps that need to be adapted to different contexts.

Index

A

Abstract Factory
  about 35
  advantages 36
  implementing 37-40
  versus, Factory Method 40
abstractmethod decorator 70

B

borg pattern 20

C

classic singleton 19
Command Pattern
  advantages 69
  disadvantages 69
  functioning 68
  implementing, in Python 70-74
  terminologies 68
  use cases 69
ConcreteCreator class 29
controller
  about 9
  recommendation 9
create_product method
  about 28
  versus, Factory method 28

D

do_something() function 44

F

Facade design pattern
  about 44
  advantages 45
  diagrammatic representation 44
  implementing, in Python 47-51
  in Pythons standard library 45, 46
  used, for troubleshooting 45
factory
  about 27
  example 28
Factory method
  about 29
  advantages 30
  implementing 30-33
Flask 10

G

get_by_short_url method 11
get_forecast method 50
get_weather_data method 47

I

isdir function 45

L

lazy initialization 53

M

model
  about 8
  recommendations 8

module-level singleton 18
monostate 20
MVC
   about 7
   benefits 10
   controller 9
   diagrammatic representation 7, 8
   implementing, in Python 10-15
   model 8
   view 8

O

Observer design pattern
   about 60
   advantages 61
   Concrete Observer A 60
   diagramatic representation 60
   implementing, in Python 61, 62
   Observer 60
   problems, solving 60
   Subject 60
   uses 61

P

parse_content method 82
parse_weather_data method 48
print_top_news() template method 84
process function 14
proxy design pattern
   about, 54
   advantages, 55
   Client interface, 54
   disadvantages, 55
   implementing, in Python, 55-58
   problems, solving, 54
   Proxy, 54
   RealSubject, 55
   Subject, 55
   uses, 55
Python
   Command Pattern, implementing 70-74
   Facade, implementing 47-50
   MVC, implementing 10-15
   Observer design pattern, implementing
      61-64

proxy design pattern, implementing 55-58
singleton, implementing 21-26
Template Method design pattern,
      implementing 79-84

R

redirect_to_full_url method 14
rm command 72

S

shorten method 11
SimpleFactory class 28
singleton
   about 17
   borg singleton 20
   classic singleton 19
   implementing, in Python 21-26
   module-level singleton 18
some operation method 29
stat.S_ISDIR 46

T

Template Method design pattern
   about, 77
   AbstractClass, 78
   benefits, 78
   ConcreteClass, 78
   diagrammatic representation, 78
   hooks, using, 79
   implementing, in Python, 79-84
TouchCommand class 71

U

Unix touch command 71

V

view
   about 8
   recommendation 9

W

WeatherProvider class 47

Thank you for buying
Learning Python Design Patterns

About Packt Publishing

Packt, pronounced 'packed', published its first book "*Mastering phpMyAdmin for Effective MySQL Management*" in April 2004 and subsequently continued to specialize in publishing highly focused books on specific technologies and solutions.

Our books and publications share the experiences of your fellow IT professionals in adapting and customizing today's systems, applications, and frameworks. Our solution based books give you the knowledge and power to customize the software and technologies you're using to get the job done. Packt books are more specific and less general than the IT books you have seen in the past. Our unique business model allows us to bring you more focused information, giving you more of what you need to know, and less of what you don't.

Packt is a modern, yet unique publishing company, which focuses on producing quality, cutting-edge books for communities of developers, administrators, and newbies alike. For more information, please visit our website: www.packtpub.com.

About Packt Open Source

In 2010, Packt launched two new brands, Packt Open Source and Packt Enterprise, in order to continue its focus on specialization. This book is part of the Packt Open Source brand, home to books published on software built around Open Source licences, and offering information to anybody from advanced developers to budding web designers. The Open Source brand also runs Packt's Open Source Royalty Scheme, by which Packt gives a royalty to each Open Source project about whose software a book is sold.

Writing for Packt

We welcome all inquiries from people who are interested in authoring. Book proposals should be sent to author@packtpub.com. If your book idea is still at an early stage and you would like to discuss it first before writing a formal book proposal, contact us; one of our commissioning editors will get in touch with you.

We're not just looking for published authors; if you have strong technical skills but no writing experience, our experienced editors can help you develop a writing career, or simply get some additional reward for your expertise.

Appcelerator Titanium: Patterns and Best Practices

ISBN: 978-1-84969-348-6   Paperback: 110 pages

Take your Titanium development experience to the next level, and build your Titanium knowledge on CommonJS structuring, MVC model implementation, memory management, and much more

1. Full step-by-step approach to help structure your apps in an MVC style that will make them more maintainable, easier to code and more stable

2. Learn best practices and optimizations both related directly to JavaScript and Titanium itself

Expert Python Programming

ISBN: 978-1-84719-494-7   Paperback: 372 pages

Best practices for designing, coding, and distributing your Python software

1. Learn Python development best practices from an expert, with detailed coverage of naming and coding conventions

2. Apply object-oriented principles, design patterns, and advanced syntax tricks

3. Manage your code with distributed version control

4. Profile and optimize your code

Please check **www.PacktPub.com** for information on our titles

Python 2.6 Graphics Coobook

ISBN: 978-1-84951-384-5   Paperback: 260 pages

Over 100 great recipes for creating and animating graphics using Python

1. Create captivating graphics with ease and bring them to life using Python

2. Apply effects to your graphics using powerful Python methods

3. Develop vector as well as raster graphics and combine them to create wonders in the animation world

4. Create interactive GUIs to make your creation of graphics simpler

Python 3 Object Oriented Programming

ISBN: 978-1-84951-126-1   Paperback: 404 pages

Harness the power of Python 3 objects

1. Learn how to do object-oriented programming in Python using this step-by-step tutorial

2. Design public interfaces using abstraction, encapsulation, and information hiding

3. Turn your designs into working software by studying the Python syntax

4. Raise, handle, define, and manipulate exceptions using special error objects

Please check **www.PacktPub.com** for information on our titles

Made in the USA
San Bernardino, CA
18 November 2014